The Symbolic Presidency

The Symbolic Presidency

How Presidents Portray Themselves

Barbara Hinckley

ROUTLEDGE
New York • London

Published in 1990 by

Routledge
an imprint of Routledge, Chapman and Hall, Inc.
29 West 35th Street
New York, NY 10001

Published in Great Britain by

Routledge
11 New Fetter Lane
London EC4P 4EE

Library of Congress Cataloging in Publication Data

Hinckley, Barbara,
   The symbolic presidency: how presidents portray themselves
/ Barbara Hinckley.
      p.   cm.
   Includes bibliographical references.
   ISBN 0-415-90267-3: —ISBN 0-415-90268-1 (pbk.)
   1. Presidents—United States. 2. Symbolism in politics—United
States. I. Title.
JK518.H56 1990
353.03'13—dc20   89-27790

British Library Cataloguing in publication data also available

Contents

Acknowledgments

Several people helped along the way as the book grew from a smaller empirical study to its present form. I would like to thank Lyn Ragsdale whose own research stimulated early thinking on the subject. John Kessel, Gary King, Murray Edelman, Lyn Ragsdale, Mark Roelofs, and Norman Thomas read versions of the manuscript. They should know that all of their suggestions were good and that some were followed. My thanks also to Karen McCurdy, Karen Hinckley, James O'Connor, and John Stein for their insights and assistance in research and coding. The Politics Department and New York University gave support, both material and intellectual. Finally, my thanks to Jay Wilson and everyone at Routledge who helped bring the book to completion.

Introduction

Symbolism forms a large and important part of political activity. It supports governments, selects leaders, and defines the terms of debate. Symbols can be used politically to shape attitudes, build support, persuade to action, or in one widely accepted definition of political power, to help A get B to do what A wants done. Writers point out that the central battle in a political conflict is often "the struggle over whose symbolic definition of a situation will prevail."[1] Control of the symbolic actions of government is as important as the control of its tangible effects.[2] Some writers go further. One calls the central political activity the symbolic manipulation of words to define situations.[3] Another says that "the theatrical staging of oneself and the situation" is "the politician's trade."[4]

All human beings use symbols, of course. Kenneth Burke calls humans "symbol-using animals," and Sheldon Messinger refers to life as theater in which a show is staged.[5] Political symbolism, then, is merely one part of this larger human activity, although an important part because its communication has an impact that is societywide.

If symbolism is central to politics, it is clearly also central to the office of President as we understand it. People speak of packaging the candidates, creating an image, managing the news. Jimmy Carter, critics say, went too far in divesting the office of its symbolic support. Ronald Reagan had talent and training from his past career that the ordinary politician does not possess. The outcome of the 1988 election, it could be said, depended on whose symbolic structuring of the situation would prevail. Consider one analysis of a "politician" for its direct, line-by-line relevance to the presidency:

> The politician is potentially always on stage. Every aspect of his behavior can become part of a public performance which must be managed and controlled to mobilize support. Many of his activities will be essentially symbolic, i.e., for the purpose of creating the desired identity in order

to draw the audience into *his* drama. It is also true that he may not be able to control the situation because he cannot be assured of audience support . . . because other performers will be competing with him and offering negative impressions of his performance, and because he may have to respond to situations not of his making.[6]

Here is the president arranging photo opportunities and meeting the Boy Scouts in the Rose Garden. The media, however, can offer negative impressions of the performance, while economic ills or foreign terrorists interfere with the action on stage.

The importance of this symbolism is well recognized. Nevertheless, what seems obvious at one level of thinking is not acknowledged at another. People compartmentalize the presidency—separating out the symbolic from all the other things the president supposedly is or does. So we speak of a president's successful image at the same time we speak of him managing the economy. The second point is as much a symbolic projection as the first. Presidents, factually speaking, do not manage the economy, but it is part of the symbolism of the office that they are singularly responsible for the nation's well-being. We speak of the president's foreign policy or economic policy, collapsing a long and complex policy-making process into the work of a single individual. We use the singular—the president—in describing what all presidents do, thereby creating the impression of specialness and incomparability. Symbolically speaking, presidents cannot even be compared with their predecessors. In short, what is recognized at one level is kept separate from what people want to believe at another level.

The same compartmentalization is seen in political science writing. Looking at two literatures—one on symbolic politics and one on the presidency—can make the point clearly. Pioneered by Harold Lasswell and associated with the work of Murray Edelman, Kenneth Burke, and others, the symbolic politics literature analyzes the use of symbols, whether in language or ritualized behavior, in giving meaning and structure to political reality. Presidential examples are used along with other examples, but they do not lead to any full investigation. The presidency is used to illustrate leadership myths, the staging of political drama, and the importance of symbols of benevolence and control.[7] In each case follow-up studies are strongly suggested, but they have not been forthcoming. Other political subjects have been studied: interest groups in the American political process, the history of the temperance movement, the symbolism of newsmaking, the theater of courts.[8] Congressional scholar Richard Fenno draws on Erving Goffman to show how House members present themselves in their districts.[9] The presidency, too, like the courts and Congress, needs a symbolic analysis.

In contrast, the presidency literature rarely cites the studies of symbolic politics, appearing for the most part unaware of their existence. Indeed, at times the literature presents as factual descriptions the same statements the other literature would use as symbolic examples. Thus, the well-known scholar Louis Koenig remarks "that the Presidency. . .has served us well is not in question. It has waged and won wars, checked depressions, spread social justice and spurred the nation's growth."[10] Note the pronoun "it" in the description. Now, of course, the presidency did not wage and win any war—the nation did. This identification of the president with the nation, chapter 2 points out, is one of the major symbolic components of the office.

The disjunction between the two approaches can be illustrated by the treatments of the concept of *leadership*. In a book published in 1964, Edelman devotes an entire chapter to the symbolism of leadership.[11] At about the same time, two other influential books discuss presidential leadership, treating it as a given and addressing the practicalities of how presidents can increase the potential implicit in the office. James MacGregor Burn's book is subtitled *The Crucible of Leadership* and Richard Neustadt's *The Politics of Leadership*.[12] Neustadt's definition of a leader's power, in persuading others to do what the leader wants done, is paralleled in the symbolic descriptions, but presidential leadership is not treated as a problem in symbolism. When Burns returns to the subject at the end of the 1970s, the symbolic politics literature is still not cited.[13] Two literatures interested in the same political subject are not meeting up with each other.

Compartmentalization is found within the presidency field as well. A growing number of writers study presidential rhetoric and the symbolism of election campaigns.[14] Many of these writers point out the symbolic implications. Elsewhere, people study presidential decision making, White House staffing, and relations with Congress. The rhetoric is kept separate from the decision making, and the symbolism from the staffing. The symbolism becomes one component of the institution that, by implication, includes other nonsymbolic components. The institution, as an example of symbolism, is not studied.

The situation can be summarized as follows: The symbolic politics literature suggests that various work on presidential symbolism is needed, but does not provide it. The presidency literature largely ignores the symbolic literature, typically taking the office at face value with its mix of symbolic and factual components. This book attempts to extend both literatures to meet up with one another. In the process, it seeks to identify key features of the institution of the presidency and trace the implications for democratic government.

Defining Symbolism

Symbol is used in its literary, not linguistic, meaning in which the object referred to has *a range of meaning beyond itself.*[15] Considered linguistically, all words are symbols—that is, the series of sounds or letters formed evoke an idea of what the word "means." In the more conventional literary usage, however, words (gestures or any series of actions) are symbols only when they call forth a larger and usually more complex set of ideas than the literal meaning of the object. As a literary symbol, the American flag evokes a range of meaning beyond that of the three-colored rectangle of silk. This larger meaning typically involves emotional, psychological, or moral content. Indeed the usefulness of symbols is that they convey the kind of meaning not easily put into words. Advertising symbols are an obvious example in which the host of good things suggested go far beyond the particular concrete image shown. Symbols are a kind of shorthand communication for a large and powerful part of human experience not otherwise easily evoked.

Symbols, further, are *socially based*: They depend on an interaction, or communication, between those giving and those receiving them. Writers point out that an object becomes a symbol when "people endow it with meaning, value, or significance."[16] Although there may be purely private symbols, with meaning only to the person using them, symbols are studied primarily, whether in art, literature, or politics, when their meaning can be shared. Thus Gusfield defines a symbol as the "multiplicity of meanings which the same object or act can have for the observer and which, in a society, are often fixed, shared, and standardized."[17] The sharing may be partial, and people may differ in the content of the symbolic messages received. Nevertheless, some common context of meaning is assumed. The society supplies the context of meaning. The American flag would symbolize different things to conventional patriots and to war protesters in the late 1960s, but the symbol may be used by either one of the groups because a shared social context exists.

Symbols also are studied primarily when they are *purposive*—that is, intended.[18] The purpose may be partly or primarily unconscious, and there need not be a perfect match between the meaning intended and the meaning communicated to others. Nevertheless, viewing symbols as communication between people, we assume some participation on the part of both the givers and receivers of the communication. Just as purely private symbols are excluded—those of interest only to the individual creating them—so are the unintended symbols excluded—those received as perceptions where no intended transmission occurred.

It is important to see that a symbolic communication *need not bear any relation to what is factually true or to what people, independently of the communication, might agree to be true.* It may bear such a relationship, but it need not do so. Sheldon Messinger refers to a symbolically "projected" self, and Erving Goffman talks of a "performance" to influence others to the way the individual would like to be perceived.[19] Other writers speak of a "presentation of the actual in terms of the ideal" or, more simply, "what people want to be true."[20] A successful communication typically evokes *what people already agree to or what they would like to think of as true.* The bottle of brandy in the advertising picture may not bring the good life that it promises. The story of George Washington's cherry tree was apparently invented by a nineteenth-century biographer by the name of Mason Weems.[21] Nevertheless, symbols have power because people would like to believe in the possibility of the good life and the honesty of American presidents.

For the society as a whole, the symbolic meaning typically evokes ideas already in the public philosophy, with the term understood as a set of beliefs characterizing the identity and history of a people, often in idealized terms.[22] Symbols evoke ideas the society wants to believe are true. The term *symbolic*, then, should not be opposed to *real*. Symbols have reality, clearly, as a projected self is seen and perceived by others and as patriotic slogans can move an entire crowd to action. They can be distinguished, however, from the literal or factual situation people might agree to in the absence of the symbolic communication. As a matter of fact the emperor was naked, but his parade was—really—a grand and glorious affair.

Hence symbols can *substitute for* something that does not exist otherwise. A wielder of symbols offers the substitute, not the wished-for independent condition: the brandy—not the good life. It is a kind of magic trick. A symbol can help produce the independent condition it stands for: so, flag-waving could be a call to action in war. But more commonly flag-waving, as one occupant of the White House seems particularly fond of, produces no further action. It is a substitute for other activity. Later chapters will show how far this symbolism-as-substitute can be carried. Presidents who are acting most powerfully are least likely to say they are one with the nation and its powers. Those who lead in the use of religious symbols—Eisenhower, Nixon—do not appear from biographers to be the most religious in private life. Those who state the nation's mission most grandly are least likely to expand its activity in the world. It follows that students of politics need to be astute symbol watchers: not only to see what the symbolic meanings are, but to judge how well the symbols correspond to the conditions they stand for.

Symbols are communicated—both given and received. In a book on George Washington, subtitled *The Making of an American Symbol*, Barry Schwartz seeks to explain how and why the legend was created. Washington was honored not only for his victories in war and politics, but for his modesty, piety, and love of country. He did not seek power for himself, so the story goes, but renounced it—twice, returning to private life after the Revolutionary War and again after service as president. Schwartz shows how Washington's virtues were well matched to the needs of the emerging republic. For a people in the throes of revolution, Washington provided a new kind of unkingly king, a democratic hero. He embodied virtues that were already prized in the country.[23] Only one component needs more emphasis in this excellent account: Washington's own role in building the legend: *i.e.*, his self presentation.

Consider the first inaugural address, the first words spoken by an American president. The speech is very short, a little over two pages in length, and almost entirely personal. Washington does not talk about the country or the very great problems it faces or what he thinks the role of a president should be. Instead, he speaks immediately about the retirement he had chosen before, explaining that the only thing that could force him to leave his retreat is duty to his country. The word *retreat* is used twice. He is aware, he says, that he inherited inferior endowments from nature. Just as he had little military ability, he feels he has few qualifications for office: so, Divine Providence, which guided the nation to victory in war, must continue to guide the nation. His piety in the speech is as pronounced as his modesty. In the one recommendation he makes to Congress, he asks the House not to pay him for his service as president. He reminds people that he had also asked not to be paid for his service in the war.

The Farewell Address is longer and more concerned with policy. Washington apparently had Madison's help in preparing it, while other portions may have been written by Alexander Hamilton and John Jay.[24] Nevertheless, Washington includes points he has made before: about his duty to his country, his inferior qualifications, and the retirement from which he had been reluctantly drawn. He returns to these themes at the conclusion of the address:

> I am nevertheless too sensible of my defects not to think it probable that I may have committed many errors. Whatever they may be, I fervently beseech the Almighty to avert or mitigate the evils to which they may tend. I shall also carry with me the hope that my country will never cease to view them with indulgence, and that, after forty-five

years of my life dedicated to its service with upright zeal, the faults of incompetent abilities will be consigned to oblivion.

With one more reference to the retreat he is looking forward to, Washington says farewell.

Washington becomes the nation's first democratic hero: literally, a legend in his own time. A practical man, highly successful, yet modest and religious, he accepts his country's honors, all the while pointing out how much he dislikes power and only desires a humble private life. People know Washington embodies these traits because he has told them he does. A symbolic communication has been given and received.

A political symbol, then, can be defined as follows:

> The communication by political actors to others for a purpose, in which the specific object referred to conveys a larger range of meaning, typically with emotional, moral, or psychological impact. This larger meaning need not be independently or factually true, but will tap ideas people want to believe in as true.

The symbols used in this communication can take many different forms: They can be words or gestures or elaborately staged events. In the drama of politics, actors, setting, dialogue, and themes of action all contribute to the total symbolic effect.

Presidents, for example, do many things to show they are president of all the people. They quote from selected letters by individual citizens, implying that they read the letters of all citizens. They avoid references to elections or voters, which might remind people that their support is partial or their mandate unclear. They fill their schedule with meetings of hundreds of carefully selected groups. They say explicitly, "I will be the President of black, brown, red, and white Americans." The symbolism is purposive: presidents want to rally as much public support as possible. It is factually incorrect. A minority of citizens, counting all eligible voters, actually voted for the person, while many voted against him. Presidents do not take time to read the letters from citizens, nor are Native Americans frequently invited to conferences at the White House. Yet, the idea is appealing not only because it gives the nation a momentary sense of community, but because it would really be quite unpleasant to think that some groups were more important to the president than others were.

To explain an appeal, however, is not to justify it. Symbols, once selected, carry on a life of their own, often outliving their original purpose. Symbols, also, can give false comfort and distract attention from problems that need to be faced. If people would like a government where red Americans have as much access to the president as white ones do, the symbolic substitute needs to be recognized and rejected. Symbols are purposive: hence we need to evaluate the intent of the symbol-givers. Symbols need to be accepted: therefore people have some control over which symbols will be the most effective ones.

We live in an age of symbolism. Magicians are at work not only in politics or advertising, but in news, entertainment, business, religion. The craft is highly regarded and rewarded, at times approaching an art form. Survival techniques are needed both by the individual and society in developing skills of symbol-identification. So, skills developed through this account of one political institution can be applied more broadly.

Symbols and Institutional Change

This symbolism has obvious importance for a study of institutions. Institutions are shaped by the perceptions and expectations of people, both those working within the institution and those working with it. Institutions, by definition, are patterns of actions and expectations that carry on over time, independent of the particular individuals or circumstances. Expectations can be shaped by organization rules and charter documents or by informal processes. Thus, if people are expected to act in certain ways—and expected to present themselves as possessing certain traits—these expectations become part of the institution, whether or not they are realistic or factually true. In the extreme case, where very few guiding rules or formal documents exist, the institution can be changed by the informal perceptions. This is especially so if the perceptions evoke strong emotional, moral, or psychological impact and are what people would like to believe to be true.

The institution of the presidency is an example of such an extreme case. The office was left open, by the writers of the Constitution, to grow with the developing nation. While the powers of Congress are carefully enumerated, no such list is provided for the presidency. The president is to "see that the laws are faithfully executed," but how this is to be done is left for presidents and others to determine. Article II of the Constitution begins: "The executive power shall be vested in a President of the United States of America." Interpreted one way, the sentence is little more than a declaration that someone called a president will head the executive branch. The president could be a figurehead. Read another way, in what has become the accepted interpretation, the sentence gives a broad, undefined authority to the office; it becomes a source of presidential power. The office is undefined; thus presidents become what people want them to be.

Congress, too, would evolve and change over the course of American history. But the changes would occur within the boundaries set by the charter document and its own substantial rules. In contrast, there are few formal rules for the president, and fewer still that carry from one administration to the next. The presidency becomes what people say it is—Supreme Court justices, teachers of the presidency, the presidents themselves.

The process becomes a dynamic one as these symbols are communicated over time. Expectations shape action; action leads to further expectations. Children learn about the president, and grow up to teach others about the office or to become president themselves. Presidents look at the public record to see what past presidents have done. It is true that public expectations can change, as points in American history call for one kind of symbol as opposed to others. Individual presidents make a difference, selecting the symbols that they find most congruous or effective. Perhaps more commonly, however, the change is more gradual and subtle. By degrees almost imperceptible, as one kind of symbol replaces another, the office is transformed.

At one point in the twentieth century, presidents were expected to say in their first inaugural what the election meant for the party and policies selected by the voters. Democrat or Republican, internationalist or isolationist, each president set forth his mandate in turn. "There has been a change of government," Wilson announced in words that would shock a modern audience. Coolidge explained, for one policy after another, what the verdict of the people was. Contemporary presidents, however, do not mention elections, much less say what an election means. When was it decided that elections were not one of the things celebrated on inauguration day? It was probably never decided, but the office—and a link between the president and the voters—had been changed.

Symbols change gradually, as new communications are given and received. So, if the office of president becomes what people say it is, we need to see what these symbolic communications are.

What the President Means to Americans

From this perspective, we can look at how people view the presidency and how they present it to others. The focus is limited to the office of president and not particular individuals in office. While these views can be contradicted at other points and by other statements, common features do emerge clearly.

Fred Greenstein explains "what the president means to Americans." The president is (1) a symbol of the nation; (2) an outlet for affect—a way of feeling good about one's country; (3) a cognitive aid, allowing a single individual to symbolize and substitute for the complexity and confusion of government; and (4) a means of vicarious participation through which people identify with the president and feel more a part of events occurring around them.[25] These perceptions are found in studies of children and adults. For the young child, the president *is* the government, with other figures viewed in relation to that basic orientation point. Congress becomes the group of people who "help the president." In other words, the president is the initial point of contact, general symbol of government, and orientation point from which the rest of the government is perceived. The president is also perceived to be both powerful and benevolent—something like the children's parents, or God. Presidents are symbols of authority and power, and they are good. Adults, like children, see the president as the primary symbol of government, give support to the incumbent in office, and see the president as the predominant political decision maker to whom others—Congress and the public in particular—are subordinate. In a study published after Watergate, most persons agreed that the president "stands for our country" and that they sleep better when a president they trust is watching over the country.[26] As children sleep better when a trusted parent is watching over them, adults, in childlike fashion, place the president in a parental role. John F. Kennedy received barely 50 percent of the vote in 1960, but by inauguration day he had the job approval of 69 percent. Gerald Ford had a similar percentage of people who approved of his job performance before he had a chance to do anything. The office, in short, is supplying support for the individual occupants.

These attitudes span years of recent American history and widely varying presidential performance. After the Watergate crisis, people wondered if the office would be permanently damaged by the scandal and resignation. In the short term, support for the presidency did drop sharply during the Watergate crisis. But support also fell for other governmental institutions, including the Supreme Court and Congress, who were in the process of checking the president in line with their constitutional responsibilities. In accord with the earlier socialization studies, the president appeared to be serving as the orientation point from which wider perceptions of government were derived. In addition, people distinguish positive views about the presidency in general from negative views about any one incumbent. People could agree that Watergate "reduced [their] confidences in the presidency," but when they were asked more general questions, no sign of that reduced confidence appeared. People said they would support the president in time of foreign or domestic crisis and think favorably of the office and its incumbents.[27] It is the office of Washington and Lincoln, not of Grant or Harding or Nixon, that the new president comes to occupy.

So when Gerald Ford assumed the presidency in August 1974, 71 percent of the public approved of the way the president was doing his job—a percentage strikingly similar to the support given presidents a decade before. After his first one hundred days in office, Carter's approval stood at 64 percent, while Nixon's had stood at a similar 61 percent after his first one hundred days. In 1976 the Associated Press reported the responses of first-graders in Salem, Oregon, when their teachers asked: "What should a President do for the people?" President should, among other things: Help ducks. Sign papers. Give poor people money. Tell people where to go. Keep people from stealing. Help a lost puppy. Help us not die. Two years after the Nixon resignation, the next generation of citizens begins to form ideas about the president's job. The president is seen as powerful and benevolent: like parents, supplying clothing, food, and shelter; and like God, watching over birds and lost puppies.

It is a very short jump indeed from these responses to adult expectations that presidents should "control the energy crisis" or manage the economy and "give us jobs." Yet these expectations follow automatically from the assumptions of power and benevolence. Studies of public attitudes show that a president's popularity rises and falls with economic conditions and with the "good news" and "bad news" reported by the press. Overall, presidential popularity (1) rises at a time of international crisis as people rally around the flag and the president; (2) declines in economic hard times and during prolonged unsuccessful wars; and (3) declines through the term from a high point in the first few months in office.[28] These findings make sense in terms of the expectations held. As symbols of the nation, presidents are supported when the national interest is threatened. But as cognitive symbol and orientation point, they are held responsible for the fortunes of government, as in the case of the economy, even when the problems are beyond their control. The same rationale helps explain the decline in support throughout the term. Since presidents do not have the power to do the things expected of them, the polls drop as the expectations are not met and the ills continue. They will rise again with the hopes and promise of a new inauguration and beginning.

These public attitudes do not develop in vacuum. Journalists, too, equate the president with the government, translating national news into "the White House story."[29] Headlines proclaim when a president makes a proposal—they do not say when Congress takes apart the proposal or substitutes a few ideas of its own. As one observer commented, "If there is a balance of powers within the government, it rarely shows on television."[30] Journalists ask candidates what they will do about inflation or the budget deficit, implying that they can do something to solve these problems. The process is circular and reinforcing. Because the president can symbolize the nation and the government, the news media concentrate on this individual in reporting the national news, thereby strengthening the symbolic connection.

Academic writers contribute to the symbolism, too. Political scientist Thomas Cronin identifies a "textbook presidency," that emphasizes the power and virtue intrinsic to the office.[31] Presidents are assumed to be powerful, frequently "the most powerful individual in the world." They are assumed to be good—indeed, to be a kind of secular high priest and moral leader for the nation. One writer describes the president as father and head of the political family, assuaging the deep-seated longings of his children. Another attributes to the president the following characteristics: humility, courage, sagacity, imagination and vision, moral convictions, nobility of spirit, and an understanding heart. A study updating Cronin's textbook presidency to the 1980s found less emphasis on power, but even more on moral leadership than was seen before.[32]

Again, the power of the nation is identified with the power of the president. If the nation is one of the most powerful in the world, then its symbol must possess the same degree of power, even though as a matter of fact the American president is more limited than most national chief executives. While many texts do not present the president in these ways, Cronin's point remains important. A substantial number of college students—and the future teachers and news reporters—are given a highly illusory view of the office.

Presidents and their advisers are subject to the same socialization. Jack Valenti, an old friend of Lyndon Johnson, describes his first view of the new president on Air Force One:

> He was in a strange way another man, not the same man I had known. I believe with others who have an intimate notion of what the presidency is all about that something inexplicable and possibly mystical takes place when a man is transported across an infinite flight of time and duty . . . to that place called the presidency.[33]

He goes on to speak of a transmutation and an alchemy. Yes, he says, he called his old friend "Mr. President," himself caught up in the mystical transformation.

An additional theme is implicit in much of the description already presented. As a single human individual who symbolizes the nation and the government, the president is alone. This aloneness leads to a curiously ahistorical view in which the current incumbent is seen apart from any recent predecessors and past events. Presidents are associated with the great figures of American history—Washington, Lincoln, and a very few others—but apart from this association they are alone. *There is only one*

President. The public shows this ahistorical view in separating their shaken confidence in Richard Nixon from their confidence in the office. Textbooks show it by describing the history of the president as the combined contributions of its greatest figures, or by reprinting the famous picture of John Kennedy standing alone at the window of the Oval Office, or by reminding readers of the plaque on Harry Truman's desk announcing "The buck stops here." A *Scholastic News Trails* teaches elementary school children about the presidency. The first page is devoted to Washington, the second to Lincoln, and the third to the then current incumbent, Gerald Ford.[34] Journalists reinforce the view with their focus on the immediate and the present. Therefore, not only are presidents pictured apart from other powerful government actors, but they are shown without predecessors. They are unique and alone.

So, reporters and citizens can criticize individual presidents or make jokes about them. Watergate becomes Nixon's failure and Vietnam is Johnson's. All the modern presidents, with the exception of Eisenhower and Kennedy, reached a point in their term where a majority of the public did not approve of the way in which they were doing their job (that is, the public said they disapproved or they did not know whether they approved or disapproved). The office, however, is not touched by the individual perceptions. Gerald Ford inherits the office of Washington and Lincoln and not the one of his predecessor. The office remains one of power and virtue no matter what particular holders of the office do.

These views about the president are not factually accurate, as a number of writers point out. Cronin speaks of the "illusory notion" that the right person in one job can solve the nation's problems. Godfrey Hodgson observes that "people confuse the power of the United States with the power of the President, failing to realize that he has only limited possibilities of harnessing and commanding the nation's resources." Theodore Lowi warns that the gap between attributed and actual power can force presidents to seek unconstitutional means.[35] The American president is considerably more limited by other political actors under the Constitution than many other democratic and nondemocratic heads of state. Congress, for example, shares such traditional executive powers as the power to tax, to make war, and to organize and fund administrative agencies. This executive, it is clear, could certainly not help ducks or save eagles without support from at least four independent and powerful congressional committees. As commander-in-chief, the president does have considerable power to issue military orders, subject to the information available, but this power would be shared by most other democratic and dictatorial heads of state. "The only power I've got is nuclear," Lyndon Johnson is supposed to have said. "And I can't use that." It is true that presidents are among the still-fairly-small group of people in the world who can start a nuclear war, but this is not usually what is meant by the power to persuade.

Problems of government continue over time. Some have their source in the international setting, some are endemic, some are so cast as to be unsolvable. Policies, too, continue over time, with much of the policy making incremental. Presidents, however, serve a maximum of eight years in office, while career bureaucrats and the average member of Congress serve considerably longer. Thus Hugh Heclo contrasts the government of strangers—the president, cabinet members, and chief advisors—with the natives in Washington—the members of Congress and the bureaucracy who watch visitors come and go.[36] In other words, presidents are not unique in the problems or limitations they face, and so may be compared with their predecessors.

Further, the presidential selection process tests many things: endurance; political skill; the ability to raise money, gain support from the party, and deal with the media. But it does not noticeably screen for altruism or "humility, sagacity, moral convictions. . .and an understanding heart." Indeed, a person with the ambition and ability to win the nomination and election would probably not be high in humility. The successful candidate must *seem* humble to appeal to a public that dislikes ambition and boasting, but that is making the symbolism explicit. An additional point should be raised, although it is more controversial. Constitutional interpretation suggests a separation of church and state. Although people may differ about how far the principle should be carried, it at least suggests that the chief political executive of the nation is not expected to be, *ex officio*, the chief religious leader.

People, of course, recognize these facts independently of their feelings about the president. The recognition, however, appears to be kept separate and does not interfere with the power of the symbolism. Two independent realities exist—the symbolic and the factually true—in views about American government.

Institutions can change with changing expectations. They can also fail or die. It is common to speak of institutions adapting to an external environment, but adaptation can take desirable or undesirable forms. If the presidency cannot be what it says it is, then we need to look more clearly at these expectations. We need to identify the symbolism of the office and the way it is carried on over time.

The studies to this point do not address the president's own activity. The institution is described by others' views about what presidents are and do. So, to take the subject further, it is important to see the presidents' own contributions to the symbolism—and the extent of convergence, or similarity, between presidents' and others' statements. If a convergence exists, presidents should present themselves

- As identical to the nation, as a symbol of the nation
- As identical to the government and the powers of government
- As unique and alone
- As the moral leader of the nation, one who can say what is good for the nation and the citizens

Most important, there should be

- A similarity across presidents in this portrayal

If the institution is shaped by what presidents and others do and say, then the similarities should be more striking than the differences. Presidents with sharply different styles and circumstances should present the office in the same way. In other words, they should be like one another in saying that they are unique.

While these components can be looked at separately, they are parts of one symbolic whole. If presidents are unique and without peer, these traits add to their attributed power. The Lonely Man in the White House is burdened—with the government *and* with the moral leadership. If the president is powerful, unique, and morally good, then the nation he symbolizes is secure in its power, mission, and morally correct course.

A symbolic meaning, it was said earlier, need not be factually true, but will tap ideas already in the public philosophy, ideas people want to be true. To the extent presidents and others advance the same views, as distinct from those that may be seen as literally or factually true, we may speak of the symbolism of the office. This is the subject of the present book—a particular view of the presidency supported by others and carried on by the presidents themselves.

1

The Institutional Context

That was the road of responsibility, that is the road we
chose, and that is the road we are continuing on today.—
Richard Nixon (economic speech)

Our Nation must not continue down the road we have
been traveling. Down the road lies the wreckage of many
great nations of the past. Let us choose instead the other
road, the road that we know to be tested, the road that
will work.—*Gerald Ford* (economic speech)

In a few days the Congress will stand at the fork of two
roads. One road is all too familiar to us. . . . The other
road promises to renew the American spirit. It is a road
of hope and opportunity.—*Ronald Reagan* (economic
speech)

As Richard Fenno studied how representatives present themselves in
their districts, this book examines how presidents present themselves and
the office to the American people. It takes the idea of symbolism as used
in the symbolic politics writing and applies it to the communication of
presidents themselves. The focus is on the modern presidency, from the
late 1940s to the 1980s, spanning presidents as different in style as
Truman and Reagan, Carter and Nixon. At times, nearly 80 percent of
the public approved of the way Eisenhower was doing his job; at other
times, nearly 80 percent disapproved of the way Truman was doing
his. Johnson faced a Congress generously supplied with a 150-member
margin of his own party in the House. Ford faced a Congress with the
same margin for the opposite party. During these years, the country
experienced times of peace and war and great domestic discord. The
presidency was said to be imperial and imperiled. Against these differences in style and political circumstances, we look for common institutional components—a particular way of presenting the office that carries
on across time.

This chapter shows what the presentations are like and how they can
be studied, and gives a first look at the institutional and political influences
at work.

Design of the Study

Presidents present themselves and the office in speeches to the nation and
more specialized groups. A public record exists for these presentations,
available to presidents and students of the presidency. Thus the public
record becomes a source and beginning point for a study of the office.

And so the idea of a symbolic presidency can be examined by (1) what presidents communicate directly; (2) what they communicate publicly, within the context of meaning found in American society; and (3) what is standardized, or shared, across all occupants of the office and not merely an individual projection. The design of the study emphasizes these three conditions.

First, it focuses on the direct actions of presidents, not those translated and filtered through media reports. Much of the research on the presidency studies the office indirectly. People look at public attitudes, media coverage, White House organization, congressional support. The subject is approached through pairings: president and public, president and press, president and Congress become tantamount to a study of the office. What is omitted in these pairings is the presidential activity itself.

Second, it focuses on public actions. Presidents do a number of things behind the closed doors of the White House—engage in briefings, make decisions, chat with friends, take naps, indulge in recreation. Some actions are more important than others to the conduct of government. But even if they could be researched, which at best would yield very partial results, such private actions are not relevant here. They are, by definition, *not* the presentations of self that presidents make to the public.

Third, the design focuses on the pattern of action that holds across presidents. An institution persists and has a life of its own beyond that of any individual members. The focus is important for another reason as well. It might be said that if speechwriters compose the speeches and advisers set the schedules, are we not studying these people's actions rather than those of the presidents? But if there are important similarities across presidents, then the particular advisers participating at any one point in time are no longer of interest. It does not matter who the speechwriter was or where he or she said the ideas came from. If the same picture is presented across presidents, the institution is carrying on specific components as opposed to other components. For example, three presidents say, "The past is prologue." It does not matter which three speechwriters suggested the phrase.

The book looks at the symbolism of the modern presidency, from Harry Truman to Ronald Reagan, through the first three years of each term. The terms for Truman and Johnson are counted as beginning with their first election; Ford is studied through 1974–75. These years are chosen to permit comparability across presidents and to avoid election-year effects. A brief analysis also compares election-year and nonelection-year activity. In fact, the third year looks quite like the fourth in the way presidents present themselves.

The public activity of presidents is listed in *The Public Papers of the Presidents of the United States.*[1] The *Public Papers*, in annual volumes, lists all presidential addresses, radio and television broadcasts, speeches to Congress, short messages, news conferences, and speeches on the road. Typically the format, subject, audience, time, and place are provided, thus giving additional valuable information. If the president addresses a group in the Rose Garden for two minutes, that message is included. An exchange with reporters at the airport is also included. All veto messages and executive orders are also in the *Public Papers*. In short, the compilation provides a comprehensive and authoritative record of the president's public and verbal activity, from George Washington to the present.

This record is limited to actions that are presidentially defined and excludes the following categories: nonpublic actions, as in White House conversations, available only through the accounts of participants; actions by other officials—such as cabinet members or White House aides— taken in the name of the administration; and purely nonverbal appearances. The first two categories are outside the design of the present book, and the third is infrequent. Apart from photo opportunities provided to journalists by the White House, most of the public appearances of the presidents are accompanied or followed by words. For example, when Lyndon Johnson travels to Uruguay for a meeting with the American Chiefs of State, he speaks at the meeting and at the airport on his arrival and departure. John F. Kennedy speaks in Berlin and on his departure and return from the trip. All these remarks are included in the *Public Papers*.

An illustration of the activity seen in the *Public Papers* is given in appendix D for the presidents through one month in office. The remarks and addresses, starred in the listing, are the major and minor speeches that will be discussed in the following chapters. The *Public Papers* includes more activities in the official list for Carter and Reagan than for previous presidents: mainly, proclamations and minor appointments. These are excluded in the present illustration. Carter makes eight proclamations in the month shown and Reagan makes sixteen, or one every other day. Reagan proclaims Mother's Day and Cancer Control Month, with a National Arthritis Month following four days later. There is also an American Indian Day, a Jewish Heritage Week, a week for farm safety, and a month for physical fitness and sports.

The month selected randomly catches presidents in various circumstances. Truman has just shocked the nation by his firing of General Douglas MacArthur. Johnson is traveling, and Carter is fighting the energy crisis. According to the Gallup polls, 68 percent of the public approve of the way Eisenhower is doing his job. Twenty-four percent approve of Truman, while support for Carter and Reagan hovers at the 40 percent mark.[2] Nevertheless, the sample shows how the *Public Papers* can track presidential activity. It also shows the curious combination of activity discussed at length in a later chapter. Eisenhower turns from the Office of Defense Mobilization to an Easter egg roll and back to the Mutual Security Program. Nixon opens the baseball season and sends a message to Congress on revenue sharing.

To measure direct activity, this book selects from the *Public Papers* all remarks delivered in person or televised live, both major and minor addresses. (All addresses to Congress and the American people were televised during the Truman administration.) Transcribed and written messages, as well as exchanges such as interviews, question-and-answer sessions, and joint remarks, are excluded. A major address is a speech before a nationwide audience: inaugural addresses and nationally broadcast speeches to Congress and the American people. A minor address is a speech delivered to a more specialized audience.

Here, then, is a public record that can be examined in a number of ways: through content analysis and a more traditional textual analysis, and by seeing the nature and timing of the speeches and the choice of audience. No one method is intended to predominate. While speeches are analyzed closely, it should be clear that this is not a study of presidential rhetoric. In showing how presidents present themselves and the government, the speeches help to identify key components of the institution.

Institutional Influences

A look at the major addresses provides a context for the following chapters while it gives a first sense of institutional effects at work. As table 1.1 shows, the average number of speeches per year remains the same across the time period. Johnson gives only one major address—the obligatory State of the Union speech–in 1966. Overall, however, presidents give about four to five major addresses a year, with the number unaffected

Table 1.1
The Number and Timing of Major Addresses

Year	1	2	3	4	Total	Average per President
Truman	3	5	4	4	16	4.0
Eisenhower	7	5	3	4	19	5.0
Kennedy	5	5	5	–	15	5.0
Johnson	6	1	4	6	17	4.0
Nixon	5	6	6	7	24	6.0
Ford	4	6	–	–	10	5.0
Carter	5	4	5	3	17	4.0
Reagan	6	7	5	4	22	5.5
Average per year	5.0	5.0	4.5	4.5		

by their years in office or by a change in presidents. (The second term average is also four for Eisenhower and Reagan, and six for Nixon. Nixon gives nine speeches in 1973 and four in 1974). No change in this area of presidential activity has occurred since the Truman years.

Presidents can give as many speeches as they like, since the networks almost always agree to White House requests for television time. Nevertheless, the speeches are in fact limited to a relatively small number. Even Reagan, with his deserved reputation as the Great Communicator, did not venture past Eisenhower's record of seven speeches in one of the first three years. Possibly presidents feel that they will outwear their welcome with the public and become too familiar to have an impact. In any case, the number of speeches appears to be limited by expectations that have developed over time.

The subject matter of the speeches is also similar, as shaped by formal rules and informal expectations. The Constitution states that presidents will "from time to time" report to Congress on the state of the union. This has come to be interpreted more rigidly with presidents since George Washington as an annual requirement and one performed at the beginning of the legislative session. When Congress convened early in September in the Madison administration, a change from its usual midwinter date, Madison delivered his annual message in September. Twentieth-century presidents, at least since Theodore Roosevelt, began to use the address not only to report on events that were occurring but to set general goals and priorities.[3] Some of the presidents, including Theodore Roosevelt and Taft, went further, giving congress a detailed list of proposals generated from the White House and the various executive departments. Contrary to popular wisdom, the practice of giving an agenda to Congress did not begin with the modern presidents.[4] Truman, however, picked up the tradition that some of his predecessors had followed, and the later speakers followed this practice.

Thus, the modern State of the Union address takes its form from expectations shaped in the White House, the departments, and the Congress. The various advisers and department heads fight to give "their" program maximum space and emphasis.[5] Congress expects presidents to supply a comprehensive agenda, even though it may subsequently disagree with proposals or substitute proposals of its own. The public expects presidents to speak for all the people, no matter what groups made up the particular winning coalition in the election. Therefore, the State of the Union message becomes a kind of wish list, much broader than a list that presidents can realistically expect to work for or that Congress can be expected to approve.[6] Truman, for example, spoke of civil rights legislation in his 1950 address, although he clearly did not expect to see it passed into law. Reagan also spoke of civil rights, even though this was probably not high on the list of priorities in the Reagan White House. State of the Union messages can be analyzed to see the different priorities of presidents; nevertheless they all share common features: They tend to be long, inclusive, and overstated in terms of the goals that can actually be achieved.

While the Constitution requires presidents to take an oath of office, all, again since Washington, have given a short address on the occasion. The precedent was so well established by 1841 that John Tyler, succeeding to office on the death of William Henry Harrison, insisted on taking the presidential oath and giving an inaugural address. Harrison was the first president to die in office, and the Constitution was not clear on the matter of succession. Would Tyler be acting president only until a special election was called? Or, if he served the full remainder of his term, would be actually be president or be merely the vice-president serving as acting president?[7] Harrison had served only one month of his term. Tyler's decision, to call himself president and to be inaugurated as such, became the first act to clarify this question of succession. Chester Alan Arthur and Andrew Johnson also gave inaugural speeches, although Millard Fillmore did not.

Twentieth-century vice-presidents succeeding to the presidency, less forced to prove their presidential credentials, have not given inaugurals. Many have given brief remarks and scheduled an address to Congress within the week. Truman, for example, gave a remark on taking office consisting of one sentence: "The world may be sure that we will prosecute the war on both fronts, east and west, to a successful conclusion." Ford gave a longer series of remarks, as we see later, but he did not call it an inaugural address. The inauguration has come to be a celebration of the democratic process, hence it is not expected at a time of trouble, at the death or resignation of a president.

Modern presidents are also expected to report to the nation and Congress on economic and foreign policy. An annual economic message and a budget message are required by law, although the message need not be delivered in person or broadcast to a nationwide audience. Most presidents in fact have given at least one economic address each year, although some combine economic policy with other subjects. The foreign policy speeches show the greatest variety of the addresses, presidents picking the particular subject they will talk about. Truman, for example, gives four speeches on Korea in 1950 alone; Johnson gives only one on Vietnam from 1965 through 1967. Carter's foreign policy speeches in the first three years all concern treaties: Panama, Camp David, and Salt II.

Given the expectations, it is not surprising that most of the major addresses—almost 90 percent—involve these four subjects: foreign and economic policy speeches plus the inaugurals and State of the Union messages. Indeed, the rare speech on another subject tends to mark administration crisis points: Kennedy on the racial crises at the University of Mississippi and Birmingham; Ford on the Nixon pardon and the energy crisis; Johnson on the Detroit riot, a steel dispute, and civil disorder. Johnson is so busy responding to crises in the two years that he does make speeches that he takes no time to address the nation on all the legislation he is moving through Congress. He does speak about the voting rights bill in his speech of 15 March 1965. The rest of the major legislation is announced only in minor addresses, ceremonies in the Oval Office surrounded by his former congressional colleagues with Johnson dispensing the pens. There are photographers to take pictures, but no television cameras in sight.

Expectations not only shape the timing and subject of the speeches, they shape their content and treatment as well. This point can be seen throughout the following chapters in the similarity—indeed, copying—from one president to another of the statements made and the particular devices employed. For the present, the point can be illustrated by a closer look at the inaugural messages.

The inauguration brings a change in government, which in many countries marks a crisis point, provoking instability and revolution. American presidents, therefore, are constrained to show, especially to other countries, that American policies will continue despite the change. Each inaugural speaker repeats the same litany of greetings:

> To our allies we say . . .
>
> To our neighbors . . .
>
> To peace-loving nations everywhere . . .
>
> To those who would be our enemies . . .

The particular words vary little from one speaker to another. The inaugural must ensure continuity, but it must also promise change, especially to the American public, whose support the new president needs. The failures or successes of the past administration must be forgotten; hopes must be renewed. Each president asserts that there can be a new beginning, ironically repeating the same words from the past. The inaugural must set forth simultaneously the themes of continuity and change. In this way the inaugural occasion and the expectations surrounding it shape the content of the addresses and their similarity to one another.

These expectations, however, do not dictate that the same words will be used or the same conventions from one president to another. The words and choices of individual presidents set new precedents and create future expectations. The invocation by clergy appears to have begun with Franklin Roosevelt at the 1937 inaugural, according to historian Daniel Boorstin.[8] All presidents since Roosevelt have followed the tradition. Eisenhower adds a prayer of his own, asking people to bow their heads. Bush picks up the Eisenhower precedent for his inaugural in 1989. Carter decides to use two Bibles instead of the one used by all presidents since George Washington. Bush also uses two Bibles. Thus the modern inaugural, expected to strike themes of continuity and change, is also expected to be a religious ceremony.

The public record, it appears, is useful not only to presidential scholars but also to the presidents and their speechwriters. The record of past speeches becomes the vehicle through which ideas and phrases are carried on across time. Some of the copying may be unconscious: witness the Republican fondness for road metaphors quoted at the beginning of the chapter. A riddle is suggested: If each Republican in turn rejects the road travelled before, how many Republicans are going in the same direction? Perhaps Carter's speechwriters did not know that their quotation from *Micah* was also used in Harding's inaugural. Ford may not have known that binding up the internal wounds of Watergate echoed Lincoln's second inaugural: "Let us strive on . . . to bind up the nation's wounds." And yet Lincoln's speeches have surfaced in at least two other modern addresses:

> Nixon: When we listen to the better angels of our nature. . . .
>
> Lincoln: When again touched, as surely they will be, by the better angels of our nature.
>
> Kennedy: In your hands, my fellow citizens, more than mine, will rest the final success or failure of our course.
>
> Lincoln: In your hands, my dissatisfied fellow-countrymen, and not in mine, is the momentous issue of civil war.

People might be reluctant to say that they have turned to this record for their own ideas, but the amount of repetition does not suggest coincidence. If this is the case, past speeches become part of the presidential institution, shaping the expectations of new office holders and their advisers.

These institutional influences need not produce the symbolic components identified in the introduction. Different presentations of the office could be chosen and carried across time. But these particular symbolic components are also shaped by expectations. If the president is expected to be a religious leader for the nation, then the choices of prayers and Bibles and religious imagery help to meet those expectations. Thus a broad set of institutional influences—from constraints on the office, the past record, and other expectations—can be seen as shaping the way presidents present the office in these speeches.

Institutional influences also shape the minor speeches, although they show more variety than the major addresses. The White House is flooded by requests for personal appearances and remarks: As a leader of all the people, the president is expected to speak to a wide variety of groups. All presidents, even George Washington apparently, had to schedule these minor remarks and appearances.[9] So, among other speeches within one year, Herbert Hoover speaks to a Methodist Council, an association of police chiefs, the YMCA and a local chamber of commerce, a union league, a Christian Endeavor society, and the Women's International League for Peace and Freedom. He gives talks through the course of a midwestern tour, addresses the Red Cross and the Gridiron Club, gives awards to aviators, and speaks at the opening of the Waldorf-Astoria Hotel.

Presidents arrange these remarks to fit their own schedules and indulge themselves in addressing favorite groups. Truman addresses the Masons four times in the first three years, while Nixon gives four speeches to football groups. Still, some groups are addressed by all presidents, and a few—Boy Scouts, the Future Farmers of America, a chamber of commerce—see the president almost every year. Reagan addresses Hoover's police chiefs, Red Cross, and YMCA, and gives awards to aviators who are astronauts. Most presidents balance their schedules to include management and labor, big and small business, and representatives of all the major religions in the country, although the particular emphasis will vary from one president to another.

The number of these addresses has increased following the Eisenhower years, but shows no further increase over time (see chapter 4). Presidents from Kennedy to Reagan give on the average about 200 of these minor speeches and brief remarks each year, or almost one every working day. Clearly, the giving of minor remarks forms one large part of the modern presidency. The remarks are shaped by expectations about the office, from inside and outside the White House, and from the record of what past presidents have done.

Political Influences

Against these institutional influences, one can compare the political effects. Institutional factors suggest similarity, and political factors, variety, given the sharply different circumstances that the presidents face. Two political factors, however, might have some importance on shaping the timing of speeches or explaining their effects. One is the president's standing in the polls, and the other is the legislative agenda in Congress. Each needs a closer look.

The Polls

The polls, as an indicator of public support, are closely watched by the White House, press, and Congress. It might be expected, then, that polls could affect the timing of speeches, and that the speeches could change the polls. Both the speeches and the polls, however, are intertwined with the most visible events of a presidential term. A dramatic event—an international crisis or trip abroad—may prompt a speech, but it may also affect the polls independently of the speech itself. Studies show that the polls are affected by economic good and bad news, by international crisis, and by other announcements.[10] Kennedy's polls jumped after the failure of the Bay of Pigs invasion; Carter's rose sixteen points when the American hostages were first seized in Iran. Neither president gave a major speech to the nation on the occasion. The polls also fall, independently of these events, from the high point in the first few months of the term. If the speeches are a cause or an effect of poll standing, they must be separated from these other events.

A study by Lyn Ragsdale helps disentangle these political effects. Looking at the discretionary speeches from Truman to Carter (i.e., excluding States of the Union and inaugurals), Ragsdale finds that a speech is most likely to occur with a change in the public opinion polls and with positive and some negative events. Speeches are least likely to occur when the polls are stable and when the economic news is bad.[11] Thus an integration crisis in a southern school prompts a speech (and a presidential action), whereas a record high for unemployment does not produce a speech. Presidents have few actions to suggest for these negative economic events. It is not clear why speeches should occur when the polls are rising. One would expect that the speeches, limited in number, would be saved for the most critical occasions. Possibly, sensing a rising tide of popularity, presidents use the occasion to push new initiatives in Congress. It is easier to explain why speeches occur when the polls are falling. Presidents must do something to correct the slide in popularity, and a speech to the nation is one action that can be taken.

Other evidence in the study also suggests that the timing of speeches is influenced by political effects. The speech itself, separate from any positive or negative events surrounding it, produces a three percentage point gain in the polls on the average compared against the months when no speeches occur. Notice that this does not mean that the speech has positive effects—it is simply less negative than not speaking. It appears that presidents judge correctly if they time their speeches to stop down-slides in popularity. The speeches marginally and at least temporarily check the downward trend.

This point can be seen more clearly by looking at the major addresses and the polls through the first three year of a president's term. These cases support Ragsdale's findings while they offer an additional interpretation and provide context for the following chapters. Public support is measured, as in the Ragsdale study, by the Gallup question, "Do you approve of the way President [name] is doing his job as president?" Given a sample error of from two to four percentage points, small changes in the polls are interpreted only if they form part of a larger pattern. The graphs of the individual presidents' polls are shown in figures 1.1 through 1.8 (pages 26–31) with a summary provided in table 1.2.

Carter's and Reagan's support is shown first in figures 1.7 and 1.8 along with their addresses and the most visible events of the time. While Reagan's speeches in the first year are followed by an increase in support, the second-year speeches show no difference or are followed by slight negative effects. Both State of the Union addresses, for example, in years 2 and 3 are followed by a slight drop in the polls. And whereas 42 percent of the public approved of the president's job performance in September of year 2, six weeks and three speeches later, 42 percent still approved. The speeches at the end of year 3 do bring upswings in the polls, but they announce events that might well bring upswings without the

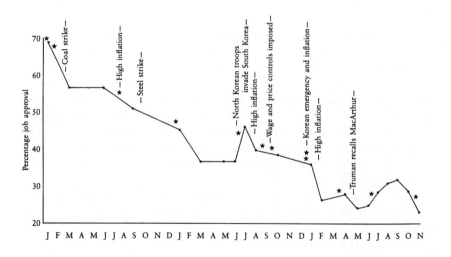

★ = speech

Figure 1.1
Harry S. Truman, 1949–51

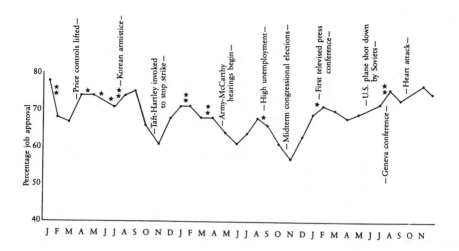

★ = speech

Figure 1.2
Dwight D. Eisenhower, 1953–55

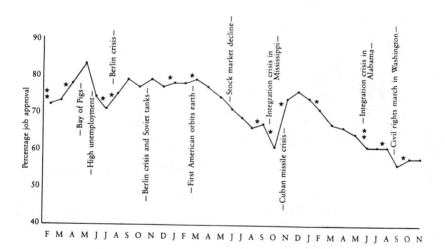

★ = speech

Figure 1.3
John F. Kennedy, 1961–63

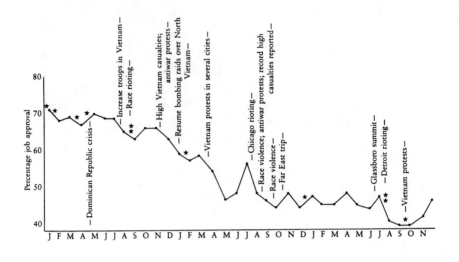

Figure 1.4
Lyndon B. Johnson 1964–68

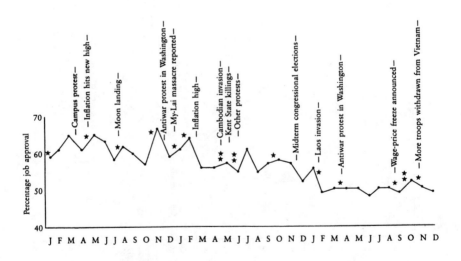

Figure 1.5
Richard M. Nixon, 1969–71

28

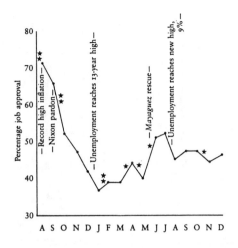

★ = speech

Figure 1.6
Gerald R. Ford, 1974–75

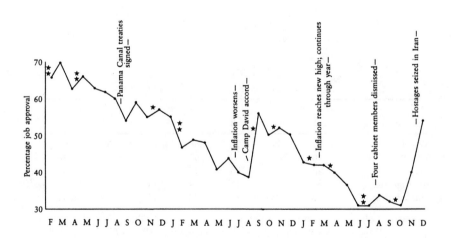

★ = speech

Figure 1.7
Jimmy Carter, 1977–79

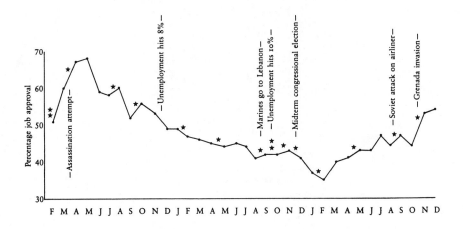

★ = speech

Figure 1.8
Ronald W. Reagan, 1981–83

Table 1.2
Presidents and the Polls: The First Three Years

Presidents	Average Poll Ratings							
	T	E	K	J	N	F[a]	C	R
Year 1	59	71	76	68	61	(55)	61	58
Year 2	40	66	73	51	57	(44)	48	44
Year 3	23	71	63	44	50	–	37	44
Average loss[b]	36	0	13	24	11	–	24	14
Maximum loss[c]	46	21	15	33	17	34	41	25

Source: Calculated from Gallup poll results in George Gallup, *The Gallup Poll: Public Opinion 1935–1971,* 3 vols. (New York: Random House, 1972); *The Gallup Poll: Public Opinion 1972–1977,* 2 vols. (Wilmington, Del.: Scholarly Resources, 1978); and later volumes of *The Gallup Report.*

a. Ford's first year is taken from August 1974 through December and his second year from January to December 1975. Taking his first twelve months in office, the average is 48 percent followed by 44 percent for August through December 1975.

b. Year 1 minus year 3.

c. The high point for the first three months minus the low point of the three years.

speeches. Both the Soviet attack on a Korean airliner and the U.S. invasion of Grenada are the kind of international event that brings the public rallying to the president's support. In focusing attention on these events, however, the speeches probably produce an additional impact. It is intriguing to see that the four occasions when the sharpest drops occur—May and November of year 1 and July and December of year 2—are also times when no speeches occur. Each is followed by a speech in the next month: two the required States of the Union and two discretionary speeches.

Reagan's popularity in the first three years is framed by two dramatic events: the attempt on his life on 30 March 1981 and the invasion of Grenada on 27 October 1983. Within this time frame, the polls fall more than twenty points. If the speeches have an affect, they can be seen primarily as slowing the downward trend, bolstering his popularity in the first year and checking its decline in year 2.

Carter's polls start higher than Reagan's and drop lower in year 3, and yet the steady downward trend is the same for both presidents. Both end the third year after a dramatic international event with 54 percent approving of the way they are doing their job. The speeches appear to work similarly also for the two presidents. Carter's addresses in April and November of year 1 are followed by poll increases, whereas his later speeches, clustered in year 3, show little difference or slight negative effects. The polls also fall slightly after both of Carter's State of the Union speeches. Other noticeable drops—March and August of year 1, April and December of year 2, and May of year 3—occur in months when there are no speeches. Arresting the trend is the dramatic Camp David accord with a speech to the nation on the occasion. Carter's polls jump back to a 56 percent approval rate and begin another decline that continues until the hostages are seized at the end of the third year.

Thus, speeches for both Carter and Reagan focus attention on dramatic international events and appear to slow an inevitable decline. Since Carter gave three speeches at the end of year 3 when his approval had fallen to a 29 percent rate, it might be said that he waited too long.

Not speaking appears to have effects for Johnson and Eisenhower, although their polls are very different (see figures 1.2 and 1.4). Johnson, who disliked television and thought that he showed poorly in front of the cameras, could not have been encouraged by the 1965 results. The speeches are followed by *decreases* in the polls; even his inaugural address shows a slight drop. The one exception is the speech marking the crisis in the Dominican Republic when the polls rise with the rally effect that one might expect. When the polls drop again after the 1966 State of the Union address, Johnson appears to swear off public speaking and does not give another major address for a year. The year 1966 would not be a good one for presidential popularity in any circumstances. Race violence and rioting erupts in several cities; major protests are beginning to be staged against the Vietnam war. Nevertheless, Johnson maintains his silence during these negative events, and the polls fall through the year until by the time of the 1967 State of the Union address they are almost twenty points lower than they were a year before. Johnson does speak after the Detroit riots and other civil disorders in July 1967, although the polls still fall with these negative events. A speech on Vietnam in September makes no difference: 38 percent of the public approve of the way Johnson is doing his job.

Throughout these years, Johnson has been signing into law one act after another of his Great Society program. Except for the State of the Union messages, however, these acts have not been the subject of major addresses. Unlike the other presidents, Johnson gives no major economic speeches, although he had more to gain and less to lose than many on these issues. Of course, it is not possible to say if another speaking strategy would have done better, but with an overall drop of thirty percentage points, it could hardly have done worse.

Eisenhower begins his term with an impressive speaking schedule. He gives eleven speeches in the first fourteen months in office and then speaks only once from the beginning of March to the end of his second year. The speeches themselves make little difference in the polls; some show no change, while some are followed by slight negative or positive turns. Nevertheless, it is intriguing how well the timing of his speeches keeps pace with his popularity. During the relatively quiet second year, the polls also decline, reaching their low point of 57 percent approval at the time of the midterm congressional elections. Again, one cannot say that the crowded speaking schedule of year 1 helped, in showing a personality or in dramatizing a time of peace and prosperity, but a different strategy could hardly have done better. It is true that Eisenhower does not speak before or after his heart attack of September 1955, and yet by the end of the year 75 percent still approve of the way he is doing his job.

Unlike Johnson and Eisenhower, Nixon times his speeches evenly through the three years, allowing no more than three months to elapse between addresses (see figure 1.5). After an initial rise in popularity, his polls decline, averaging 61 percent approval in year 1, 57 percent in year 2, and 50 percent in year 3. Still, the cluster of speeches from April to June of 1970 is interesting. During this time the Cambodian invasion occurs, followed by widespread protests across the country, and the killings at Kent State. The polls that bracket these speeches and events show very little change, from 56 percent approval in mid-April to 55 percent in mid-June. Another cluster of speeches, from August to October of year 3, also shows no change in the polls, with Nixon's support holding at 50 percent. Several of the months when he does not speak—January to March, July–August, and November–December of year 2—do show drops in the polls, although the period of April to July of year 3 shows no change. One could make an argument on the circumstantial evidence that Nixon timed his speeches to minimize the negative effects of war protests and elapsing time. Through three years of widespread and vocal protest at home, his own support fell only about ten percentage points. The story of Nixon's popularity is not over in 1971, but for the time he has done better than many other presidents in limiting his losses through the first three years of the polls.

Kennedy's polls appear more closely linked with external events than with occasions of speaking and not speaking. His initial high popularity climbs even higher with the Bay of Pigs incident and remains above 70 percent approval through the first year (see figure 1.3). Kennedy gives no speeches between August and the end of the year, but his support does not fall; presumably he is helped in part by the continuing crisis in Berlin, as Soviet tanks move to protect the Berlin Wall that is cordoning off the eastern sector of the city. Between March and August of year 2, when he gives no speeches, his support falls in continuing small increments a total of twelve percentage points. The polls fall further with the integration crisis at the University of Mississippi, although Kennedy gives a speech on the occasion. Then, however, the Cuban Missile Crisis intervenes, bringing the nation to what some considered the brink of nuclear war. Kennedy's successful handling of the crisis regains his support, and he finishes year 2 with a 76 percent approval rate.

Kennedy's polls in year 3 begin to look more like the polls of other presidents. Support declines through the year: ten percentage points from January to May when he gives no speeches; three more percentage points with the racial violence in Birmingham and Governor George Wallace's refusal to permit black student to enroll at the University of Alabama. A civil rights march in Washington, led by the Reverend Martin Luther King, Jr., is followed by a further drop in support. During this time Kennedy speaks twice on civil rights and twice on his controversial nuclear test ban treaty. By September 1963, he has fallen for the first time in his term below a 60 percent approval rate. Unlike Nixon, Kennedy's speeches do not appear to be geared to helping his popularity. Of the speeches not directly responding to events, one has been an economic speech and the other three were part of his fight for the nuclear test ban treaty.

While the polls in the beginning of Truman's term are not reported frequently enough to judge the effects of speeches or events, the broad outlines can be seen in figure 1.7. Truman's support disintegrates long before the Korean war, it is important to notice, falling thirty percentage points by June of year 2. After a brief rally point at the onset of the war, the polls continue to fall, although Truman gives three speeches between July and the end of the year. The new wage-and-price controls he has introduced are controversial and debate is widespread on the conduct of the war, both on how limited and how extensive the American response should be. Some people oppose the use of American troops in Korea; others believe that the war should be carried to the Chinese Communist mainland. Even before Truman relieves the popular General Douglas MacArthur of his command, only 28 percent of the public approve of how Truman is doing his job. The polls fall four percentage points further after the action, which is accompanied by another speech on the war.

The decline in the latter part of the term is not surprising, given the controversy and the economic constraints. But the plunge in the first eighteen months remains unexplained. There are labor strikes, it is true, and high inflation, although the strikes have lessened from the immediate postwar years. It is also true that between his inaugural and the next State of the Union address, Truman has given only one address to the nation. At the same time, he has been fighting his own Democratic Congress and trading punches with the press. No president could be less concerned with his own popularity than Truman; so perhaps the polls are merely mirroring and giving back this lack of concern.

If speeches had an independent positive effect, Ford's polls would look quite different. He speaks early and often, giving a total of ten addresses in seventeen months in office (see figure 1.6). Ford's speeches, however, are primarily directed at damage control. His speech announcing the pardon of Nixon brings a fourteen percentage point drop in support. His one foreign policy speech occurs with the fall of Cambodia, and the annual message to Congress says that the state of the union is "not good." The remaining speeches primarily concern problems of the economy. The *Mayaguez* incident, involving the use of American troops to rescue a merchant ship and its crew, brings the one upswing of support in his term. This event, however, is not accompanied by a speech. Given the negative news that Ford has to impart, his speeches appear effective. Only the speeches on the pardon and the fall of Cambodia are followed by decreases in the polls; the others show no difference or positive effects. Indeed, his support in December 1975 is only four percentage points lower than it was after the Nixon pardon fifteen months before. Damage control is not a popular subject, and yet 46 percent of the public could approve of the way Ford was doing his job.

While Ford's speeches are not directly comparable with the other presidents because of his shorter term, they do illustrate features common to all the modern presidents. Events *(Mayaguez)* can produce a rise in support without speaking, while other events (the Nixon pardon) bring a decrease whether or not a speech is given. Speeches seem most effective as a form of damage control: They can counter some negative events, producing no difference in the polls; and they can slow the normal downward trend. Thus, it becomes clear why speaking shows a small positive effect overall. It is not that the speech is so persuasive but that the silence can hurt.

The point is important as context for the following chapters where we see the kind of presentations made in the speeches. If the speeches had positive effects in themselves, the choice of presentation might be important. But it is more likely that these addresses would have the same effect no matter what presentation was made. It is the speech itself, not its content or style, that is important. The results for the three-year terms are similar to Ragsdale's reported earlier: Speaking versus not speaking makes a difference of almost two percentage points, significant at the .01 level.[13]

The results also suggest some political advice for bolstering public support (see table 1.2). Speak early and often (Eisenhower, Nixon) rather than rarely (Truman, Johnson) or late (Carter). Think about increasing the number of speeches compared to the presidents of the past. Given the usual downward trend[14] shown in the table, the risk of familiarity may not be as great, or as well founded, as the risk of silence.

The Legislative Agenda

Speeches may be made with an eye toward the legislative agenda, presidents selecting subjects of highest priority or those needing the public to bolster congressional support. Presidents give about the same number of discretionary speeches, however, no matter how ambitious their legislative program or what they can expect from Congress. A look at the subject of the speeches, too, shows more similarity than differences.

One category of discretionary speeches has nothing to do with legislation. That is the response to events as seen in the previous section: the commitment of troops, announcements of summits, speeches on civil disorders, and others. Whether they are intended to highlight positive events or provide damage control for negative ones, all presidents use some of their limited number of speeches for these occasions.

A second category of discretionary speeches are broad statements of policy and goals: economic speeches that accompany a more detailed message to Congress, some of Carter's speeches on energy, many of Eisenhower's speeches. These may be intended to help the agenda by creating public support and a sense of a president who is in charge of the nation's problems. The polls, however, do not show any clear positive effect, nor is the public being told what they should ask Congress to do.

A final category of speeches do ask for legislation, perhaps one-third of the discretionary speeches altogether. Kennedy speaks three times for a nuclear test ban treaty. Johnson introduces the voting rights bill, and Nixon speaks for a Supreme Court nomination. Carter argues for the Panama Canal treaty and Salt II, while Reagan asks for congressional support for the Nicaraguan *contras*. Several presidents propose tax plans, and give follow-up economic speeches listing the legislation that they still need passed. It is interesting that the greatest number of these follow-up economic speeches listing the legislation that they still need passed. It is interesting that the greatest number of these follow-up economic speeches are given by the Republican presidents Nixon, Ford, and Reagan. Facing one or both chambers controlled by Democrats, the Republicans do seem to be using these speeches to rally greater public support. Nixon gives three of the speeches, Ford five, and Reagan a total of seven.

The speeches point to subjects of high priority in each administration: Kennedy's test ban, Johnson's voting rights, Reagan's budget and tax proposals. While some of the proposals are more likely to succeed than others, all are controversial, and all, it could be argued, are worth the president's lobbying effort. Overall, the greatest number of these speeches are given in years 2 and 3, the time when the battles with Congress are well under way. The totals, excluding Ford's speeches, are four in the first year, nine in the second, and eight in the third year. More of the speeches are given by Republicans than Democrats, although the differences are slight. The Republicans on the average give slightly more than one such speech a year, and the Democrats give slightly less than one.

Clearly, some of the speeches appear to be made for their legislative effect, although they constitute only a small proportion of all the major addresses. At the same time, many other high-priority agenda items are not given separate speeches, referred to only in State of the Union messages. It is also difficult to say if the speaking has an effect: While some of the legislation is passed—the test ban treaty, the voting act—more is defeated or heavily compromised by the Congress. Since presidents are expected to fight for their legislative program, the speeches may be most important in showing White House concern. Not speaking, which produces negative reaction in the polls, might also produce a negative reaction in Congress.

The timing and subject of speeches can be influenced by political factors, both the polls and the state of legislation in Congress. Yet, the similarity of the speeches across presidents argues that the primary influences are institutional. Presidents are expected to make a certain number and kind of speeches each year. They are also expected to respond to events, both positive and negative, to remind the public that the president is in control, and to fight for their program in Congress. Understanding this institutional context is important in understanding the following chapters. The major addresses do not vary greatly from one president to another. It appears that presidents follow the past record not only in the number and subject of the speeches but in the kind of presentations made.

This book, then, utilizes the public record to understand a particular institutional dynamic—a set of expectations surrounding the office that can be called the symbolic presidency. It asks how presidents present themselves and the office to the American public, in the major and minor addresses described in this chapter. The audience of presidential speeches gains an overall impression merely, or what might be thought of as a series of pictures of government. How many actors, for example, are shown at work in the government? How are they characterized, and what kinds of things do they do? What, in other words, does the government look like, and what is the president's place, relation to others, and characteristic activity? It is this overall impression, or pictures of government, that the following chapters seek to discern. Thus chapter 2 looks at the main factors featured in the major addresses; that is, what the government is said to be. It also shows how the setting, in rearranging time and American history, adds to the overall effect. Chapter 3 continues the analysis of major addresses, examining the kind of activity projected. It asks what the job consists of—what presidents say they do. Chapter 4 extends the investigation to the minor addresses, looking at the subjects and audiences chosen and the effects of the audience. As presidents schedule their minor addresses, they say more about the range and nature of the presidential job. Chapter 5 traces the process of institutionalization back into history and shows how distinctive the modern presidents are. A final chapter brings the results together to identify the symbolic presidency and ask about the future of the office.

2

Pictures of Government: The Actors

[This is] a government of laws and not of men.—*John Adams* (incorporated into the Massachusetts Constitution, 1790)

What is good for the country is good for the President and vice versa.—*Richard Neustadt,* Presidential scholar

Speeches are the major form through which presidents present themselves—and the government—to the nation. Who, then, are the actors in this political drama, and how are they portrayed? Presidents share policymaking authority with a decentralized and powerful Congress. They head an executive bureaucracy of enormous size and diverse, often conflicting, points of view. They act in a political context along with other powerful individuals: in their own and the other political party, in organized groups across the nation, and in state and local governments. Moreover, much of the policy they are involved in making lies beyond any national government's control. Decisions taken by other heads of state, in the international economic community, or in the private sector profoundly shape the options available in foreign and economic policy spheres. How much of all this do presidents convey in their presentation of governing activity? It is clear from public opinion studies that citizens see the president as the government. When other actors are identified at all, they are cast in subordinate roles. To what extent, then, do presidents contribute to this erroneous impression in their descriptions of the government?

It is important also to see the consistency across presidents. Popular writing emphasizes the differences in personality, style, and circumstances; some academic literature supports this view as well. According to this view, each presentation should be sharply distinctive: Kennedy's presentation would not be the same as Nixon's, nor Nixon's the same as Reagan's or Ford's. A second argument also suggests that the differences should outweigh the similarities. Pictures of government might be shaped by traditional differences between the parties or by agenda priorities. Hence some presidents might be more willing than others to mention Congress, administration actors, or particular groups. Republican presidents might be different from Democratic presidents, and legislative activists unlike the less active presidents. Alternatively, the way government is presented may be similar for all presidents, independent of party, priorities, or circumstance. A basic institutional component of the office would be carried on by the presidents themselves.

This chapter, therefore, should help explain what influences coming from the White House shape perceptions about the president and the government. The chapter begins with an analysis of the presidential figure, as presented in the sentence subjects, the connections made throughout the speeches, and the repetitions used across presidents. It then looks at how other actors are presented and the particular devices employed. It is not only the president but Congress, groups, and citizens who are characterized in the same way and through the same forms. A final section shows how the setting in time and space adds to the characterization and brings a new dimension to the office.

The Presidential Nation

The first dominant impression, seen consistently across the years, is the president's identification with the nation and the American people. It is not only the public that sees the president as symbol of the nation—the presidents themselves are encouraging this view. As table 2.1 shows, the major actors in government are the president, the nation, and the American people, together constituting three-fourths of the subjects used in the inaugurals and economic addresses and nearly two-thirds in the foreign policy speeches. The primary actor, however, is none of these three taken alone or added together, but the collective pronoun we." The word becomes a way of saying that president, nation, and people are synonyms and may be used interchangeably. The effect is created as "we" weaves its tortuous path through the speeches.

Eisenhower makes the following three statements in his inaugural:

> We are called as a people to give testimony . . .
>
> For all our own material might, even we need markets in the world . . .
>
> Respecting the UN . . . we shall strive to make it . . . an effective force

The first statement is clear and the second probably refers to the nation, since the people themselves do not need markets or possess material might. The third is more difficult. Eisenhower has been listing the principles of faith by which we (the people) live, but the sentence by itself suggests that the Eisenhower administration or the U.S. government will try to make the United Nations an effective force. Reagan's statements in his inaugural address are similar:

Table 2.1

The Major Government Actors (Sentence Subjects) in Presidential Addresses

Presidents (Truman to Reagan)	Percentage of Subject References[a]								Total (all presidents)
	T	E	K	J	N	F	C	R	
Inaugural Addresses									
Actor									
I, this administration	12	3	8	13	23	63	16	15	17
The nation, United States	5	0	0	2	4	3	3	2	2
The American People	5	5	10	2	0	3	8	2	4
We	60	63	35	49	51	10	63	58	52
All other actors	18	24	47	34	22	21	19	23	25
N subject references	65	63	40	47	79	30	38	59	421
Economic Addresses									
Actor									
I, this administration	28	37	30	–	38	43	31	27	32
The nation, United States	1	0	1	–	2	3	0	1	1
The American people	5	10	3	–	5	6	3	5	5
We	29	47	33	–	38	36	51	43	40
All other Actors	37	6	33	–	17	12	15	24	22
N subject references	196	62	86	–[b]	201	159	101	501	1306
Foreign policy addresses									
Actor									
I, this administration	11	–	30	23	37	34	19	14	23
The nation, United States	3	–	4	2	1	8	1	1	3
The American people	1	–	2	0	3	2	–	1	
We	45	–	34	37	31	32	42	32	39
All other actors	39	–	30	38	29	24	38	52	37
N subject references	299	–[b]	134	81	216	161	74	239	1204

a. A Subject reference indicates any human reference (people, nations, or institutions) used as the subject of the sentence, with each sentence counted once. The first subject only of compound sentences is counted. Rhetorical references to hypothetical people ("someone might say"; "a critic could argue") are omitted. For a full listing of the categories used and coding, see table 2.3 and appendixes.

b. No addresses to the nation were given in these categories in the three years.

We, the Americans of today, are ready . . .

We are a nation under God . . .

To those neighbors and allies who share our freedom . . . we will negotiate . . .

The point is that the particular nouns referred to do not matter, since each can be used as a synonym for others.

This device is not merely the traditional "royal we," used when leaders pluralize themselves to equal the government. When Shakespeare's King Lear says, "We have divided in three our kingdom," the pronoun refers to the royal Lear. The presidential device, in contrast, not only includes the government but extends to the nation and the people as the basis for the government. Moreover, it is distinguished by its lack of clear reference and shifts of meaning. Frequently, the context is so confused that it could refer to any of these actors or more than one. Typically the word is used in several senses and without clear referents within the same paragraph.[1] Thus, by the deliberate blurring and blending of the word "we," an effect that can be termed *symbolic equivalence* is established. The word links the president with the public and the nation and further equates administration proposals with public and nation. It becomes a means of enlisting support for specific proposals because, literally, they are said to be synonymous with the nation and the American people.

Examples of this device, found in all speeches from Truman to Reagan, are worth quoting at some length. Eisenhower speaks on 15 March 1954 about the tax program before Congress: "You and I tonight [addressing the American people] will be discussing. . . . We recognize, of course, that taxes are necessary. We know that through taxes our Government gets the money to carry on its necessary functions." After this enlightening beginning, the pronoun subjects shift quickly: "I know how burdensome your taxes have been and continue to be. So we are watching every expenditure of Government. . . . But while we are insisting upon good management . . . we have, at the same time, asked the Congress. . . ." Within one page, we the people becomes we the Eisenhower administration.

On 13 August 1962, Kennedy argues for points in his domestic program still not passed by Congress: "We need enactment of our bill to provide for youth employment opportunities. You know today that we have in this country one million boys and girls who are out of school and out of work. In the next eight years of this decade, according to some predictions, we are going to have eight million boys and girls. . . ." We the administration becomes we the nation. Reagan points out, on 24 September 1981, that "we [the administration] propose to dismantle two Cabinet Departments, Energy and Education" because "we [the nation or the American people] don't need an Energy Department to solve our basic energy problem."

The same equivalence is employed in the foreign policy speeches. In explaining the situation in the Dominican Republic, Johnson moves from "we in this hemisphere" to "we [the administration] have acted" to "we" as the United States, and back to the administration proposals. Reagan informs us that "two hours ago we [the administration] released the first photos from Grenada" and that "we [the nation] got there just in time." Truman begins his 15 December 1950 speech on the Korean action with one reference to "our nation, all the things we believe in" and one reference to what "we" in the administration have accomplished in the past five years.

While the examples have shown only specific passages, the effect carries to the speech as a whole. As the single most frequent subject of the sentences, the pronoun becomes the unifier of the entire action whereby presidents simultaneously (1) invoke national pride and patriotism, (2) appeal to the American people for support, (3) show the people that they are one of them, and (4) propose and explain actions of the administration. As we the nation shifts to we the people and back again, presidents remind their audience of their democratic office: They are at the same time one of the people and a leader of the people. Moreover, this symbolic equivalence is found not only in the sentence subjects; the pronoun shifts meaning within a sentence, thereby blending even more thoroughly the action being portrayed. So, Reagan concludes his address to the nation on a tax reduction proposal (27 July 1981):

> Our struggle for nationhood, our unrelenting fight for freedom, our very existence—these have all rested on the assurance that you must be free to shape your life as you are best able to, and that no one can stop you from reaching higher or take you from the creativity that has made America the envy of mankind. . . . In these six months, we've done so much and have come so far. It's been the power of millions of people like you who have determined that we will make America great again. You have made the difference up to now. You will make the difference again. Let us not stop now.

The syntax may be confused, but the symbolism is clear. Claims for the nation's greatness and its very existence are linked to the efforts of the first six months of the Reagan administration, invoked by a president who is speaking as one of the American people and simultaneously asking the American people for support. Reagan can be clear when he wants to be. In a speech to conservatives quoted in chapter 4, the word "we" has only one meaning—it refers to the conservative group.

The device forms a major structural component of the speeches, linking the major actors and presenting them as one. The speeches discuss the nation's foreign policy stance or economic needs. They give lengthy descriptions of the people's spirit (Nixon), sense of covenant (Johnson), or principles of faith (Eisenhower). Nevertheless, the nouns describing this nation and people are rarely used as subject—altogether about five percent of the time. As the percentage breakdown in table 2.1 makes clear, the star of the government drama is "we."

This symbolic equivalence is used by all presidents through the twenty-five years and in all three kinds of speeches. In the inaugurals, with only one exception, use of the plural far out-numbers the singular, whether "I," "the president," "this administration" or a synonym. The same pattern is seen in the economic and foreign policy speeches, although in somewhat less extreme form. Since these addresses require policy statements about what the administration has done and intends to do, it is difficult to avoid the singular entirely. Still, even in these more factually oriented addresses, the plural overpowers the singular and specific: 52 percent compared to 17 percent in the inaugurals, 40 compared to 32 percent in economic speeches, and 39 compared to 23 percent in the foreign policy speeches.

The one exception is interesting. Gerald Ford uses the singular more than the plural in his "Remarks on Taking Office." The one nonelected president does not make the symbolic identification that the other presidents do, but he has not called his address an inaugural either. The case is less exception than support for the presidential rule. Ford's reluctance to use the symbolic plural carries over to the economic and foreign policy speeches. In a speech to Congress on 10 April 1975, Ford fights for a foreign aid bill that Congress had substantially revised. The former minority leader of the House makes several statements about the power of the president to make foreign policy. He asserts that the "executive must have flexibility in the conduct of foreign policy" and that the president is "entrusted by the Constitution with primary responsibility for the conduct of our foreign affairs." But while he makes these statements about presidential power, he is reluctant to claim the power in the phrasing of the speeches. He refers to himself personally and to the country as the United States; the other presidents usually call the country "we."

Other minor variations can be seen in table 2.1. Nixon, for example, is somewhat more willing to use the first person singular than the other presidents. Kennedy is exceptional in citing other actors in the inaugurals (primarily references to other nations) and Eisenhower for not citing them in economic speeches. Still, the similarity across presidents is more striking than the differences. When presidents address the nation, it is America speaking.

Overall, no differences are found for party, time period, or electoral status in the frequency with which presidents cite any other actors. Truman, Johnson, and Ford, who came to the White House through succession, are no more likely to cite other actors than the rest of the presidents are. In other words, they are as willing as the other presidents to present themselves along with the nation and the American people as the single major actor in the government. Democratic presidents refer to other actors only slightly less frequently than Republicans do. The postimperial presidents, Ford, Carter, and Reagan, are like their predecessors in their willingness to dominate the action described in the speeches. The comparisons follow:

	Reference to All Other Actors (percentage of sentence subjects)
Democratic presidents	31
Republican presidents	26
Presidents by succession	28
All other presidents	27
Postimperial presidents	26
The five earlier presidents	28

Exceptional Speeches

As Ford's inaugural illustrates, the use of the plural is discretionary: It is chosen by presidents over other forms as the way to present the office. The point can be seen more clearly by looking at the other exceptional cases where presidents have chosen not to use this device; one, by Ford again, announcing the pardon of Nixon; a second, by Kennedy on 12 May 1963, reacting to racial violence in Birmingham, Alabama; and a third, by Johnson on 3 September 1965, announcing the settlement of a steel strike. All mark exceptional occasions, requiring presidents to react to unique events for which no clear tradition exists. All are also short speeches. The presidents respond to the event only and do not discuss larger goals or problems.

Ford is concerned with making two points: (1) that he personally believes that the pardon of Nixon is the morally right thing to do; and (2) that, right or wrong, he has the power to do this as president. Almost every sentence in this short speech of 39 sentences is directed to one of these points. Fourteen sentences express religious or moral sentiments: God is referred to five times and conscience six times. Fourteen sentences also make reference to the presidency or the Constitution (some of these overlap with the religious sentences). Ford refers to the Constitution three times and to himself as president eight times. He uses the phrase "domestic tranquility," speaks of the decisions that come to "this desk," and says, quoting Truman, that the buck stops here. Despite this emphasis on the office, the plural pronoun is never used, and the singular is used seventeen times. Other sentence subjects include the American people, friends, and courts, each used once. Ford is clearly speaking as a president, but as an individual president who has made a decision. The focus of the action, and the responsibility, is clear.

Kennedy's speech is very different from Ford's; it is even shorter, factual, and very formal. He uses legal phrases, refers to both parties in the dispute, the accords, agreements, and statutory obligations. Again, however, there is no use of the plural, seven instances of the singular pronoun, and three references to this government, the federal government, or an official of the government. Again, also, Kennedy is speaking as president, announcing the order he is taking and stating what the federal government is prepared to do: "This government will do whatever must be done to preserve order, to protect the lives of its citizens, and to uphold the law of the land." Kennedy states that he will send federal troops to Birmingham and will nationalize the Alabama National Guard. In this conflict over enforcing a national law, the focus is on the national government itself and the actions taken in the name of that government by an individual president.

Johnson's speech shows a third variation. He announces a peaceful settlement of a steel strike, bringing the representatives of union and management along with him on the platform. The speech itself reflects the multiple actors who are featured. The industry, union, and management are the subjects eleven times; the country three times; and Johnson six times with five uses of the pronoun "I." Johnson gets his steel settlement, and the negotiating representatives get praised by the president for their service to the country.

All three cases show presidents engaged in an exercise of power in domestic politics. Ford and Kennedy are announcing automatic self-executing orders, while Johnson reports a victory already achieved. In these cases the presidents might feel that they do not need to borrow power from a symbolic equivalence with the nation—they can speak in their own name as president. Ironically, then, the presentation of the office would be at its grandest when presidents are most weak, and most concerned with appealing to the public and Congress for support. The point remains speculative. It does not hold for the foreign policy speeches where presidents speak as commander-in-chief. These speeches show the same presentation as the most controversial economic proposals. Truman's firing of Douglas MacArthur, for example, is buried at the end of a foreign policy speech that explains what we, the president and the nation, must do in Korea. Nor is it clear what effects, if any, this change in presentation makes. Ford's polls fall sharply with the Nixon pardon, but Truman's polls also fall with a very different presentation. Kennedy's and Johnson's polls remain high and show no difference compared to other speeches in the same period using different presentations. In any case, these examples show that presidents can vary their presentation if they want to. Yet they remain the rare exceptions in the addresses.

One can now begin to see the convergence between presidents and others in the ways they present the office. Presidents, as well as presidential scholars, equate the president with the nation. Thus, Louis Koenig says that the presidency has waged and won wars, and Richard Neustadt remarks that "what is good for the country is good for the president and vice versa."[2] Presidential actions are both a result of, and an influence on, a set of expectations about the office. Presidents respond to these expectations in American society and at the same time carry them on for future generations. One component of these expectations is clear: The president not only represents the nation and the public but becomes them. They are the same and interchangeable.

The Other Actors

Beyond the president, the nation, and the ubiquitous, evershifting "we," few actors play major roles. The frequencies are reported in table 2.2. Just how totally the president dominates the action—in his symbolic identity with the nation and the citizenry—can be seen clearly from the table. The second most frequently appearing actor is cited only 9 percent of the time in the inaugural addresses, 8 percent in the economic speeches, and 19 percent in the foreign policy speeches. Most of the time attention is focused on the president alone.

The inauguration, of course, is the president's ceremony, and such domination can be expected. But even in other major addresses the same pattern is seen. The point is most sharply outlined in economic speeches. While presidents are not alone in making economic policy, they appear alone in the addresses. References to other economic actors—in Congress, in the international economic community, or in the private sector—rarely appear. The Council of Economic Advisers or other economists are cited as subject in no sentences, while the Federal Reserve is cited only twice. If Congress fares badly with only few references, the president's cabinet and advisers fare even worse. In economic addresses, the cabinet or individual cabinet members are the subjects in only seven sentences, while all other administrative units or officials are the subject in nine. New units that the president proposes to establish are the subject in eight more.

In foreign policy, also, presidents give the impression that they act alone. Administration advisers, including the secretaries of state and defense, ambassadors, joint chiefs and other generals, are rarely mentioned, totaling only 3 percent of the subject references overall. In all of the foreign policy speeches, the secretary of state is the subject four times,

Presidents (Truman to Reagan)	Percentage of Subject References[a]								Total (all presidents)
	T	E	K	J	N	F	C	R	
Inaugural addresses									
Actor									
We, the President, and the nation[b]	82	76	53	66	78	79	90	77	75
Congress	0	0	0	0	0	0	0	0	0
Administration, advisers	0	2	0	0	3	0	3	5	2
Subnational groups	0	2	0	11	1	0	0	7	3
Other nations	9	17	35	2	4	0	3	2	9
Humanity, the world	9	2	13	13	11	0	5	0	7
All other actors	0	1	0	8	3	21	0	9	4
N subject references	65	63	40	47	79	30	38	59	421
Economic addresses									
Actor									
We, the President, and the nation[b]	63	94	67	–	83	88	85	76	78
Congress	7	0	2	–	1	6	3	11	7
Administration, advisers	3	3	2	–	5	2	5	6	4
Subnational groups	20	0	22	–	5	3	4	5	8
Other nations	1	0	0	–	1	0	1	0	0
Humanity, the world	1	0	0	–	1	0	0	0	0
All other actors	5	3	7	–	4	1	1	2	3
N subject references	196	62	86	–	201	159	101	501	1306
Foreign policy addresses									
Actor									
We, the President, and the nation[b]	61	–	70	62	71	76	62	48	65
Congress	1	–	0	0	0	2	1	2	1
Administration, advisers	4	–	2	5	2	4	0	1	3
Subnational groups	4	–	0	5	4	0	0	5	3
Other nations	23	–	23	9	11	15	32	25	19
Humanity, the world	0	–	1	0	0	1	0	2	1
All other actors	7	–	4	19	11	2	4	16	9
N subject references	299	–[c]	134	81	216	161	74	239	1204

a. Subject references are selected as explained in table 2.1 Congress includes all congressional references—to the institution, members, or groups. Administration includes all references to any executive agency or member, formal or informal presidential advisers, or references to "the government" or "government." Subnational groups may be broad—"farmers," "the unemployed"—or specific, as in a particular interest group. The category also includes American soldiers. The final residual category includes all other human subjects mentioned. For fuller details on the coding, see appendix B.

b. Combined total from the first four rows of table 2.1, for each category of addresses: the president speaking in the first person singular or plural, or references to the nation and the American people.

c. No addresses to the nation were given in these categories in the years under study.

ambassadors five times, joint chiefs three, and other generals three. Other participants—the secretary of defense, a vice-president, special negotiators, the Central Intelligence Agency—each appear three times or less. Other nations and governments are talked about, making foreign policy appear less presidentially dominated than the other addresses. But *the action includes almost no other American participants.* The other Americans mentioned are primarily soldiers fighting or American citizens with sons killed in battle. The point is worth emphasizing, since foreign policy speeches attempt to invoke national pride and patriotism. Nevertheless, the only dramatic focus supplied for the emotion is the president himself. It is no wonder that the public rallies behind the president in time of crisis, as studies of public opinion show. Not only is the president the chief symbol of the nation, he is the only one.

Take the example of Truman's second speech to the nation concerning Korea, on 1 September 1950. He describes the history of communist aggression in Korea and points out how fiercely the South Koreans are fighting for their freedom. He describes the current lines of battle and details the countries contributing troops to the United Nations forces, mentioning more than thirty countries altogether. He concludes:

> Against the futile and tragic course of dictatorship, we uphold, for all people, the way of freedom—the way of mutual cooperation and international peace. We assert that mankind can find progress and advancement along the path of peace. At this critical hour in the history of the world, our country has been called upon to give of its leadership. . . . We have responded to that call. We will not fail.

The structure of the action is clear and sharp, as seen in the sentence subjects. We, the president, and the nation are the subject in about sixty sentences, while other nations are the subject in approximately thirty. American troops comprise most of the remainder, leaving only five other American references.

Reagan combines Lebanon and Grenada in his speech of 27 October 1983. He gives the background to the Middle Eastern conflict and tells stories about a Lebanese mother, an American father waiting for news of his son, and a general and a dying marine. He gives facts and figures on the country of Grenada and its history over the past four years. Citing names and places, he explains the military coup that occurred. He goes on to describe what the attacking U.S. forces found, the size of the Cuban military force, and the number taken prisoner. As commander-in-chief, he praises the American military who planned and carried out the campaign. He then turns back to a discussion of Dominica, Grenada, Lebanon, and the Soviet Union.

Many observers felt that the invasion of Grenada was an attempt by the Reagan administration to divert attention from Lebanon and the heavy American casualties there. The swift and successful action in Grenada could restore support for the administration and patriotic morale. The speech seems designed to create the same effect. We, the president, and the nation are the subject in about fifty sentences, while other nations are also the subject in about sixty. American troops and soldiers are the subject in almost thirty more, leaving six references to other American subjects. After the stories and the complicated details of two conflicts in different parts of the globe, people might only remember the scrawled *semper fi* of the dying machine.

Nixon supplies the same amount of detail in a speech on Cambodia. On 3 June 1970 he explains the past five years of Cambodian history, counts the number of South Vietnamese and Americans that took part in the attack, and names the weapons confiscated. He shows Defense Department film of the captured war material:

> And now you are looking at some of the heavy mortars and rocket launchers and recoilless rifles that have shelled U.S. base camps and Vietnamese towns. We have seized over 2,000 of these along with 90,000 rounds of ammunition. That is as much as the enemy fires in a whole year. . . . And here you see rice, more than 11 million pounds of rice. . . .

In contrast to all this detail, the American government is portrayed simply. It is the president speaking.

The foreign policy speeches include military milestones in recent American history: the Korean war, the Cuban missile crisis, the bombing of Cambodia, sending the marines to Lebanon. People may rally around the president in time of international crisis, but the speeches make clear that presidents are doing much of the rallying themselves. Against a threat from abroad that is described in detail, the president is the only American buttress along with the people, the nation, and the American soldiers fighting. Any patriotism or other emotion aroused by the speech is given no focus except the presidents and their policy proposals.

The same use of detail is seen in the economic speeches where facts and figures are cited heavily. Presidents use charts, graphs, and detailed statistics to explain inflation and unemployment trends. Cost-of-living spirals and complicated tax proposals are explained at length. Kennedy brings charts with him to explain trends in the gross national product, industrial production, and disposable personal income. Reagan gives a speech (16 August 1982) that consists almost entirely of (1) a review of past interest rates and unemployment percentages, (2) an explanation of the prime rate, and (3) projected changes in revenues under the proposed tax bill. He explains:

> Revenues would increase over a three-year period by about $99 billion, and outlays in that same period would be reduced by $280 billion. Now, as you can see, that figures out to be about a 3-to-1 ratio—$3 less in spending outlays for each $1 of increased revenue.

Presidents are not trying to be entertaining in these speeches. Thus it is not all detail, but only the detail on the government that is lacking. Attention is directed from the tax charts and the reconnaissance photos to the solitary figure of the president.

Throughout these addresses—inaugurals, economic and foreign policy speeches—Congress appears active primarily in planning or returning from its adjournment. It does not oppose the president—it merely goes home. This characterization is made by all presidents, whether of the same or opposite party as the congressional majority, and whether, as in the case of Johnson and Ford, they had spent long years as congressional leaders. Thus Nixon and Kennedy remind the American people that "Congress has adjourned," and Ford says flatly, "The Congress has gone home." The same characterization is used in speaking of legislation past or pending. Carter speaks of legislation that Congress passed "before recessing," and Reagan lists what should be done before Congress goes home. Richard Fenno describes how members of Congress separate themselves from the congressional institution, criticizing it in their own presentations in the district.[3] Presidents, it seems clear, run against Congress, too. Always a minor character on the presidential stage, Congress is also a lazy one, never fully at work on the business of government.

The device is seen most frequently in the legislative-agenda speeches described previously. So, Nixon reviews his economic proposals that are still pending, repeating the phrase, "It is time for the Congress to act." Ford reminds his audience of the severity of the energy crisis and the urgent need for his program. Like Nixon, he echoes the refrain, "What did the Congress do in March about energy? . . . What did the Congress do in April? . . . What has the Congress done in May about energy? Congress did nothing and went home for a ten-day recess." Ford's adoption of the device is particularly interesting. In his first speech to Congress shortly after taking office, the former minority leader recalls his long years in the chamber, reminds his audience that he knows how much Congress can do when it wants to, and even calls it the "coequal branch." Within the year, however, he is engaged in a pitched battle with the

Democratic Congress. Vetoes and overrides fly back and forth between the White House and Capitol Hill. Ford soon adopts the traditional terminology of presidents: If Congress returns from recess after hearing from you, Ford tells the American people, "we will soon get back" on the right road.

In none of these cases is there the suggestion that Congress might not *like* the president's proposals or that it might be hard at work on proposals of its own. Inaction is merely laziness or worse. And so Americans must suffer the energy crisis while Congress goes off for a ten-day recess. If this is the way presidents lobby for their proposals, they are clearly not lobbying the Congress directly. At least, the portrait they are painting is not one to curry favor or influence votes.

Presidents do vary their references to other actors, as table 2.3 suggests. Kennedy emphasizes other nations in his inaugural, while Johnson begins his War on Poverty by concentrating on domestic groups. Ford divides attention between himself and references to the Nixon family. The foreign policy speeches also vary in the extent that presidents feel they must describe the actions of other governments. Nevertheless, the similarities in the table are more striking than the differences. Other participants in the government rarely appear.

State of the Union addresses, not included in the table, show much the same pattern. They are a kind of combined inaugural and policy address. Like the inaugurals, they strike themes of patriotism and hope and set general goals, but they also review specific policies and describe new proposals. The typical State of the Union address mentions most of the major areas of government activity, each given its own paragraph or few sentences. Truman, for example, mentions health, labor, education, natural resources, highways, agriculture, social security, housing, and civil rights, in addition to longer discussions of foreign policy and the economy. Even Reagan has his list of the things that government must pay attention to: in 1983, education, trade, technology, civil rights, criminal justice, state and local governments, health, agriculture, and employment, in addition to foreign policy and the federal deficit. The federal deficit has been a subject in these speeches since 1953.

A selection of State of the Union addresses was examined for each president, using the third year of the first full term in office. "All other actors" beyond the president, the nation, and the American people constituted 24 percent of the subject references, comparable to the speeches shown in table 2.1. The distribution of these references is also similar to the other addresses and can be compared directly with the results in table 2.2:

	Percentage of Subject References
We, the president, and the nation	76
Congress	2
Administration, advisers	3
Subnational groups	7
Other nations, governments	9
The world, humanity	1
All other actors	2
N = 1441 references	

Groups are cited with similar frequency to that found in the economic speeches, and other nations are mentioned as frequently as in the inaugurals, though less than in the foreign policy addresses. Congress is cited as infrequently—even though the State of the Union is delivered to Congress—as in the other addresses.

There are exceptions. In one State of the Union address, Nixon invites Congress to make history, with the refrain "This can be the Congress" repeated six times. Carter also includes many congressional references in two speeches, although not as the sentence subjects. Overall, however, the congressional audience does not change the presidential presentation. The members gathered to hear the address are given an initial pleasantry, as presidents speak of a deceased colleague or recall their own days in Congress. Occasionally they hear the word Congress mentioned as when Carter says he will ask Congress, he will propose to Congress, and he will call on the Congress; but, by and large, they are not being flattered by their role in the government. Juxtaposed against the long list of things that the government must do, the president stands alone.

Journalists are often criticized for ignoring the separation of powers, giving the public the misleading view that presidents make policy alone. It is clear from these results that presidents present the same picture. One gains little sense of a government—complete with advisers, congressional committees and leaders, cabinet secretaries and ambassadors—at work in the domestic or foreign policy sphere.

Citizens and Groups

Further consistency is seen by looking at the people who play minor parts in the addresses. These tend to be highly stylized symbols rather than specific political actors in a real-world situation. A closer look at three devices in particular, found consistently across presidents, illustrates the point: (1) the description of interest-group politics; (2) the device of the citizen letter writers; and (3) the other individuals who appear briefly (the final row of table 2.3) for walk-on parts on the presidential stage.

Groups represent different interests in American society, frequently opposing one another. They lobby both president and Congress to bring government policy more in line with their own position. Nevertheless, one gains no sense of this activity from the presidential addresses. Subnational groups are cast in broad symbolic categories: businessmen, the unemployed, American soldiers fighting. Moreover, they tend to be cast in combinations—wage earners and the unemployed; the old and the young; business, farmers, and labor—broad enough to serve as synonyms for the American people as a whole. Thus, Nixon says that he has consulted with "scores of representatives of labor and business, of farmers and consumers, of the Congress, and state and local government" and that they agree inflation must be fought here and now. Kennedy combines taxpayers, businessmen, and workers, and Carter joins "every business, every nation, every professional group, every individual." Reagan speaks of young couples, older Americans, small businessmen, and parents; Ford combines the "farmer in Iowa, the housewife in California, the retired couple in Florida, the small businessman in New Jersey, the student in Texas, all of you." Therefore, the group references shown in table 2.2 overstate the role of these participants. They are less independent actors in their own right than synonyms for the public at large. They become symbolic equivalents for the American people, already identified with the president, and suggest the unity of the people rather than their divisiveness.

Subnational groups specific enough to suggest political conflict almost never appear as subject. The only exceptions in either the inaugural or economic addresses are Truman's mention of cattlemen, growers and feeders and retailers, Nixon's military and civil employees of the Armed Forces currently out of work, and Reagan's yacht owners, commercial vessels and airlines. Truman is the only president to mention a lobbyist by name in any reference, and not only as sentence subject, when he mentions the National Association of Manufacturers. This lack of specificity is particularly striking in the economic speeches where other kinds of details are supplied so readily. The effect is to keep the actors on stage to a minimum. The effect is also to reinforce the unity of the American people in their association with, and support for, the president.

One subnational group that clearly suggests divisiveness and conflict is discussed at length in the following chapter: the political party. It is sufficient to say here that, with only one exception, a reference to "Republicans and Democrats in Congress," the words referring to parties, Republicans or Democrats, used singly or in combination, do not occur in any of these speeches as the subject of the action. Even the exception combines the two parties and relegates them to Congress. Presidents spend much of their addresses describing policies. But the description does not include the activity of interest groups or political parties, the positions of specific interests, or the nature of the conflict that must be resolved.

Citizens are shown by all presidents through the device of the citizen letter writer.[4] Thus, Reagan cites a letter from "a wife and mother named Judith, who lives in Selma, Alabama." She writes, "Dear Mr. President: It's 3:45 A.M. and for over an hour I've been unable to sleep. . . . After years of training and experience, we can't find jobs. . . ." Truman reads letters about inflation from a homemaker in Brooklyn, and a seventy-nine-year-old in Cincinnati; and Kennedy quotes worries about unemployment from a sixty-three-year-old in Eau Claire; a young couple in Davy, West Virginia; and a fifty-two-year-old in Carbon County, Pennsylvania. Nixon says: "Thousands of letters have come to this desk since I made the announcement of the wage-price freeze seven weeks ago. Listen to what people all across America, from all walks of life, have written to me, the president, about this program." He then reads excerpts from a widow in New Jersey, a wage earner in New York, the wife of a government employee in Texas, and a worker in Oregon.

Subnational groups are cast broadly so as to symbolize the American public at large. Through the device of the letter writer, these groups are given specific names and localities, evenly distributed by age, sex, and region, to suggest all the citizens. Nixon spells it out. They are people "all across America, from all walks of life," and they write to him, the president. Presidents thus show they represent all the people, by these broadly distributed examples, and that they are a leader of the people, by the thousands who write to them in their anxiety and sleeplessness. Even as presidents argue for a controversial economic program, opposed in Congress and by specific groups in the nation, the actors cited in support of the program are the American people, both groups and individuals, who the president cares for and represents.

Again, notice that presidents are not alone in suggesting this paternal care for their American flock. Political scientist Fred Greenstein remarks that presidents serve as an outlet for affect and may, for a portion of the population, become a father surrogate.[5] An American government textbook cited in the previous chapter described the president as a father responding to the "deep-seated longing" of his children. Indeed, the idea may have found expression well before modern times, as a statement from an 1898 textbook suggests:

> The President is the head of the nation, the chief magistrate, the common father of the people, to whom they write when in trouble or deeply moved, to whom they feel they have a right of personal access as primitive in its simplicity as if the office were still a tribal chieftainship,

a busy man of affairs, with so many things to attend to that there do not seem to be hours enough in the day for them all.[6]

The president in 1982, Ronald Reagan, who reads the 3:00 A.M. letter from the sleepless citizen is expressing the same idea as the 1898 text. If the president is seen as the common father of the citizens, burdened with the care of his children, they will call on him when they are worried and cannot sleep.

The other actors reinforce the symbolic association of the president with the American people and the nation. Those most frequently cited are God, American founders or great presidents, and letter-writing citizens. In a total of twenty-one references in inaugural addresses, God is mentioned seven times and presidential greats (Washington, Jefferson, Lincoln, and Franklin Roosevelt) six times.

Other references are to an American soldier killed in battle (three times), "American heroes" generally (once), and the Apollo astronauts (once). Johnson refers to "the next President," Reagan mentions Carter, and Ford mentions Nixon. Of forty-three references found in all the economic addresses, nearly half are devoted to the letter writers or other examples of American citizens, followed in frequency by references to presidential greats and to God. Of the remainder, there are two references to Winston Churchill, one to Alexis de Tocqueville, two to the boxer Joe Louis, and a general reference to our past leaders. The only specific economic actors mentioned are the Federal Reserve or its chairman (twice) and, once each, the National Association of Manufacturers, a task force in the private sector, and Alice Rivlin of the Congressional Budget Office.

All References

The same results are seen for all references used in the addresses. Table 2.3 shows the frequency of all American actors mentioned in inaugural and foreign policy speeches, whether the actors are individuals, groups, or institutions.[7] The results, it is important to see, closely parallel the findings for the sentence subjects. References to "we," "the nation," and "the American people" show by far the largest frequency, followed by references to "I," "the President," and "the current administration." All references to other American actors total only 12 percent in the inaugurals and 24 percent in the foreign policy speeches. Even these, however, include a large proportion of references to American soldiers, reinforcing the idea of national strength and the patriotism of the American people. Excluding American military forces from the category of all other actors leaves an overall percentage of 12.[8] Many of the remaining are the citizen letter writers and groups that add up to the American people.

Table 2.3
All References to American Actors: Inaugural and Foreign Policy Addresses[a]

	Percentage of References Inaugural	Foreign Policy	Total
We	72	51	63
I	15	25	20
All other	12	24	17
Soldiers	(1)	(10)	(5)
Other actors	(11)	(14)	(12)
	(99%)	(100%)	(100%)
N references	876	654	1530

a. All nouns or pronouns used as nouns are counted for all American actors, individuals, groups, or institutions. References are counted as many times as they occur in the sentence, with the following exceptions: Quotations or letters of citizens are counted once for the author, and names with titles are counted once; for example, Speaker of the House Thomas "Tip" O'Neill is counted as one congressional reference. The coding by categories follows the scheme set forth in table 2.3 and appendix B. All inaugurals and a sample of foreign policy speeches are coded as follows: speeches of 15 December 1950, 22 October 1962, 2 May 1965, 3 June 1970, 18 September 1978, and 20 September 1982.

The results are the same for a sample of economic speeches not shown in the table. Of the 25 percent of the references to all actors beside the president, most refer to groups in combinations: workers and the unemployed, the old and the young, businessmen and consumers, those more fortunate and less fortunate. Excluding these combined groups leaves slightly less than 5 percent of the references to all other American actors, including those in Congress and the executive branch.[9]

A picture of American government begins to come into focus. It centers on a dominant presidential figure who is one with the nation and the American people. Presidents act alone, with few reminders of Congress, the executive bureaucracy or the divergent interests of interest groups. When other actors appear—the citizen letter writers, the old and the young—they tend to be highly stylized figures, less real-world actors than symbols of the nation and the public, already identified with the president. Washington and Jefferson appear briefly on stage during appeals for tax reform or budget cuts, to remind the audience of America's past greatness, while Apollo astronauts and black sports champions carry the past promise to the present. In this particular portrayal of government, presidents make policy alone after reading their letters from sleepless Americans and thinking about what is best for all the people: wage earners and the unemployed, business and labor, the young and the old.

This picture, moreover, is strikingly consistent across presidents, spanning twenty-five years of American history. It is similar in the relative frequency of actors and the symbolic equivalence established. The similarity carries even to the specific devices: the combined groups, the vacationing Congress, the letter-writing citizens. Some presidents work more with the Congress or the Cabinet than others, but this variation is not shown in the public portrayal. Presidents differ in the party and group interests they represent, but these differences do not appear, since the parties and groups do not appear. The same picture is carried—even copied—from one president to another through the speeches.

A later chapter will place these patterns in clearer perspective. In contrast to the modern speakers, the earlier twentieth-century presidents show great variety in how they present the government. Overall, they are less likely to refer to themselves as the nation and more likely to mention government and interest groups. However, one finds a variety of models to choose from. Speeches show personal leadership (Franklin Roosevelt), policy leadership (Theodore Roosevelt), and a carefully separated and divided government (Taft). The speeches vary in the kind of self references made and the number of other actors mentioned. The modern patterns, therefore, are not a rhetorical artifact—any necessary or obvious consequence of speech-making. The presidents appear to be choosing some forms of presentation and discarding others.

Individual Differences

This institutional component can be distinguished from the differences in individual style. Truman's speeches, with their short sentences and single-syllable words, match the style he cultivated in office. Here is the straight-talking man of the people. He says flatly: "We have to keep prices down. This is hard to do. . . . The problem is going to be with us for two more years at least." And he adds: "These are the facts. I am not coloring them one way or the other." Even the letters he reads have the same style. ("I am a homemaker. My husband earns a fixed salary.") Eisenhower's style, with its many abstract nouns and long sentences, is directly opposite. He begins his inaugural: "Before I begin the expression of those thoughts that I deem appropriate to this moment, would you permit me the privilege of uttering a little private prayer of my own." He describes the economy: "The productivity of our heads, our hands, and our hearts is the source of all the strength we can command for both the enrichment of our lives and the winning of the peace." These are short sentences for Eisenhower—many others are a paragraph in length.

Nixon, like Reagan, uses a colloquial style with many concrete examples. He reads letters, intersperses conversational phrases, and seems to make a conscious effort, not found with many of these speakers, to hold an audience:

> Let me put it this way . . .
>
> Here is what I will do . . .
>
> Ask yourselves this question . . .

The contrast between the speech and the formal appearance of the man on the television screen led one critic to wonder if it did not create distrust.[10]

Whether or not Carter is deliberately trying to distance himself from Nixon in his speeches, he certainly achieves this effect. Carter gives lectures, marked by long sentences and fewer concrete facts than most presidents supply. Where Nixon has said, "Here is what I will do," Carter says, "I want to discuss with you tonight some of the approaches we have been able to develop." Or where Nixon announces, "I have appointed a Pay Board," Carter says, "I've directed a council of my regulatory department and agencies to coordinate their regulations, to prevent overlapping and duplication." Although he says many of the same things that the other presidents do, an unfortunate negative effect lingers. Truman's "hard choices" and Eisenhower's "tax burden we willingly share" become for Carter "difficult and unpleasant decisions." Other presidents admit that their economic proposals will need the support of all citizens. Truman, for example, says: "I can't do the whole job by myself. This is something the whole country should support. It's up to all of us." In contrast, Carter's proposals are followed by the words: "If, tomorrow or next week or next month, you ridicule them, ignore them, pick them apart before they have a chance to work, then you will have reduced their chance of succeeding."

The negativism is not limited to the economic addresses. The Middle East peace treaty between Israel and Egypt, signed at Camp David, is a high point of the Carter administration and a major achievement for any president. And yet the point in the speech that acknowledges his role is buried between negative statements: "It was this stalemate and the prospect for an even worse future that prompted me. . . . It's impossible to overstate. . . ."[11] Carter's negative statements are also his shortest ones and the most emotion laden, standing out from the rest of the neutral discourse.

The one consistency in style is that each president differs sharply from his predecessor. Reagan is as far from Carter as Carter is from Nixon and Ford. To stand apart from the Eisenhower prose and Kennedy's formal style, Johnson is supposed to have said to his speechwriters, "I want four-letter words, and I want four sentences to the paragraph. Now that's what I want you to give it to me."[12] Nevertheless, the differences in style do not affect the presentation of the office. Reagan's letter writers do not sound like Truman's, but they are used in the same way by the two presidents. There is an institutional component, operating from the White House and carrying on over time, independent of the individuals in office.

Setting

Elements of setting add their own effects to the characters portrayed. The actual setting, of course, is ceremonial and abstract, focusing attention on the president and the prestige of the office. Addresses are made from the White House or the Capitol, structures highly imposing in their own right and traditional symbols of the government. Inaugural addresses are typically made from the east front of the Capitol (one was given from the west front and one from the East Room at the White House). Economic addresses are given in the Oval Office almost without exception; and foreign policy speeches in the Oval Office, the president's own office in the White House, or the White House theater. Against this physical backdrop, both the staging and the television cameras focus on the president alone. The setting is stark and abstract, with the only objects appearing the presidential seal or other symbol of the office. Thus the setting reinforces the characterization in portraying the president without other government actors and identifying the president with symbols of the nation.

The same effect is conveyed by what the presidents say in their addresses—and what sense of the physical world is conveyed. This too is abstract and lacks detail. Physical place references, like human references discussed earlier, are absent or limited to famous battlefields or other heroic occasions in American history. The two exceptions, where presidents go to some length to give a sense of setting, are themselves worth quoting. In his inaugural, Reagan points out the place where he is standing:

> Directly in front of me, the monument to a monumental man, George Washington, father of our country. . . . Off to one side, the stately memorial to Thomas Jefferson. . . . And then, beyond the Reflecting Pool, the dignified columns of the Lincoln Memorial. . . . Beyond these monuments to heroism is the Potomac River, and on the far shore the sloping hills of Arlington National Cemetery, with its row upon row of simple white markers. . . . Their [soldiers buried in Arlington] lives ended in places called Belleau Wood, the Argonne, Omaha Beach,

> Salerno, and halfway around the world on Guadalcanal, Tarawa, Pork Chop Hill, and the Chosin Reservoir, and on a hundred rice paddies and jungles of a place called Vietnam.

The speech effectively moves from the president at the center to the person directly in front of him—George Washington—to other presidential monuments and Americans killed in battle. It moves progressively from the Capitol steps to the surrounding city and halfway around the world. The effect is to capsulize and invoke the greatness of American history from the president to an extended periphery of the world. While the detail supplied is exceptional, the effect is similar to the other addresses in maintaining attention on the president and on his identification with the nation.

The other case—and the real exception—occurs in Johnson's inaugural: "Think of our world as it looks from that rocket that is heading toward Mars. It is like a child's globe, hanging in space, the continents stuck to its sides like colored maps." Johnson uses the imagery to call for peace and say that "there is world enough for all to seek their happiness in their own way." Nixon echoes the point, presumably consciously picking up the theme from the preceding inaugural, giving a view of earth "as the Apollo astronauts flew over the moon's gray surface on Christmas Eve." This shift in perspective contrasts sharply with the bipolar world view of the preceding presidents, where the world, when it is referred to at all, is divided between free and communist nations. The shift, however, is not continued. Ford and Carter give virtually no physical description, and Reagan brings us back to the national center and surrounding world as a battlefield of American soldiers.

These shifts in perspective should not be overstressed. The main point, and the major effect created, is the lack of such perspective and physical detail. The abstractness of the actual setting—with the president alone and the seal of office—is repeated in the abstractness of the setting conveyed in the presidential rhetoric.

The same abstraction and lack of detail is carried to the setting in time. It is worth asking, on the basis of the speeches given, what events in American history have occurred and what are the recent experiences and problems of the office. How, in other words, do presidents present themselves and their administration in relation to the past?

The history is as vague as the geography. First, few specific events of American history are cited, and these tend to be the highly symbolic ones. Excluding the inaugurals of Ford and Reagan and Reagan's economic speeches, no president makes more than five references in all the speeches in a category (i.e., all economic speeches, all foreign policy speeches) to a specific American historical event. The references that are made focus almost entirely on four presidents—Washington, Lincoln, Jefferson, Franklin Roosevelt—or on allusions to the American Revolution, the 1930s depression, or twentieth-century wars. Scattered references are made to settlers and immigrants, one to blacks gaining in opportunity, and one to the Apollo astronauts. In the exceptional cases, Ford alludes to Watergate and the resignation, and Reagan describes the nation's economic history.

Second, there is almost no recent past. Excluding the Ford and Reagan speeches referred to earlier, presidents average one reference apiece to a recent administration in all the speeches in a category. (That is, they average one reference for all economic policy speeches and one reference for all foreign policy speeches.) Truman mentions Franklin Roosevelt once, and Johnson refers once to the Kennedy assassination. Reagan speaks of "building on the Camp David accords," but does not mention that they were Carter's accords and not his own. Just as *Scholastic News Trails* told the elementary school children about presidents Washington, Lincoln, and Ford, so the presidents collapse the office to themselves and occasional references to four great presidents. In 195 pages of major speeches, all twentieth-century presidents, excluding Franklin Roosevelt, are mentioned only ten times. The four presidents—Washington, Jefferson, Lincoln, and Franklin Roosevelt—are mentioned twenty times.

In this case, individual and party differences are evident, ranking speakers by the number of past presidents they name. Reagan is the leader, with speeches accounting for half of all the historical references. He mentions all four great presidents as well as former office-holders Carter, Truman, and Theodore Roosevelt. Ford follows Reagan in ranking and is followed in turn by Nixon and Eisenhower. No Democrat makes more than two references to past presidents in all his major speeches in the time period, and Kennedy, in fact, makes no references. Just as Kennedy has struck the theme for a new generation of Americans, Reagan strikes the countertheme, reminding his listeners of the greatness of the nation's past.

It is interesting that the Republicans are more willing than the Democrats to mention presidents of the past, including the name of Franklin Roosevelt. While this traditionalism might be expected from the more conservative party, another effect may be also at work. Since Republicans typically need more bipartisan support from Congress than Democrats do, the compliments to past Democrats may be well calculated. Reagan refers to Truman, for example, in a 1983 speech explicitly calling for bipartisan support for Nicaraguan aid. Since Truman needed Republican help for his European Recovery Program, Reagan is calling on the Democrats to return the favor.

A closer look at the inaugurals shows other differences. Kennedy continues to be the least historical. He only briefly refers to "our fore-bears" and the American Revolution and makes one mention of a twenti-eth-century war. Reagan in contrast gives his own summary of American history, complete with the Declaration of Independence, Washington, Jefferson, Lincoln, and ten references to twentieth-century wars. The predominant impression is one of American fighting. Nixon deliberately shifts the time frame, balancing past and future to center on the present moment:

> Each moment in history is a fleeting time, precious and unique. But some stand out as moments of beginning, in which courses are set that shape decades or centuries. This can be such a moment.

From this perspective he looks back to the great strides in science that have occurred in the past century and to the growth of government power. He looks ahead to the American bicentennial and the third millen-nium. The only president mentioned is Franklin Roosevelt. Just as the Roosevelt era marked a critical change in American history, the new administration can bring another such change. In each of these cases, the time frame appears consciously constructed to convey a sense of the tone and style of the new administration. In other words, when speakers give their own highly selected account of American history, they appear to know what they are doing.

Despite the individual differences, the overall effect is clear. There are few reminders that other presidents have recently stood in the same place, said many of the same things, and faced the same problems. The recent past is blotted out along with the recent presidents. Everything is made new.

This sense of new beginnings—of an ever fresh, newly created pres-ent—is the third important finding of the chapter. The present is new, the future holds ever more promise, and the past is forgotten, even deliberately discarded. This theme, as other writers have pointed out, is central to the American myth and is not limited to presidents. As James Robertson describes it, "American is a fresh place, a new beginning, an opportunity; it *is* the New World."[13] The American Revolution is the charter myth, Robertson continues.[14] According to the myth, the revolution created a new nation and erased the past; hence, we celebrate the spirit of the nation by a continual process of creation and erasing. Or as Frances FitzGerald summarizes in *Fire in the Lake*,[15] "Americans ignore history, for to them everything has always seemed new under the sun. . . ."

This same emphasis on new beginnings is found throughout the presi-dential addresses, although the inaugurals, as one might expect, show the effect most clearly. Each president sounds the same theme:

Truman: We will advance . . .

Kennedy: Let us now begin . . .

Johnson: Let us seek to go forward . . .

Nixon: Let us go forward . . .

Ford: We must go forward now . . .

Reagan: Let us begin . . .

Everyone knows the Kennedy lines "the torch has been passed to a new generation of Americans," but few know the equally striking words of Johnson:

> For this is what America is all about. It is the uncrossed desert and the unclimbed ridge. It is the star that is not reached. . . . Is our world gone? We say farewell. Is a new world coming? We welcome it, and we will bend it to the hopes of man.

Carter is exceptional in admitting "I have no new dream to set forth today, but rather urge a fresh faith in the old dream." And yet even he asserts that "Americans can be better. We can be even stronger than before." He goes on to speak of "a new beginning, a new dedication within our government," and closes with words echoing the other recent presidents of "the ever-expanding American dream."

Reagan's genius for re-creating the American past can be seen in this perspective. If Reagan's past is a movie, as some writers assert,[16] then movies can take the place of the past: American history can be recast to an improved Hollywood version. So, a program of volunteerism is cast in the spirit of an old-fashioned barn raising, and a modern election campaign becomes a whistle-stop tour. Reagan thus brings to a higher level—both more instinctive and more professional—the process of re-creating that all presidents pursue.

These effects have important implications for the way citizens view the government. Concentration on the current incumbent, to the exclusion of the past, obscures the fact that some problems cannot be solved in one administration. When all hopes are pinned on the present incumbent, disillusionment must follow when the unrealistic hopes cannot be fulfilled.[17] Here we see that the presidents themselves are carrying on this impression. Recent history is irrelevant. Everything can begin anew. Further, in associating themselves with Washington, Lincoln, and Jefferson, and not the recent presidents, even the relatively popular ones, they give the impression that it is not a problem of *government* they are involved with, but a carrying on of a patriotic spirit and a cultural tradition. We see the burying grounds of Americans killed in battle and national monuments, but we lack detail about the real, though unheroic, world of the past and present. Murray Edelman points out that setting can heighten the perceived competence and stature of the actor by excluding the environment of real-world problems and concerns.[18] The setting conveyed in presidential speeches shows this effect most clearly. There is only one president offered for attention and one symbol of the nation, with no sense of continuity except the ever-expanding American dream.

Thus the setting in time and space reinforces the effects of the characterization in (1) strengthening the identification of the president and nation; and (2) focusing attention on the president alone, without the distractions of real-world government, other political actors, or the recent past. Viewed across time, the effect is humorous, as each president repeats the words that now we can really begin. But beneath the repetition lies a serious point. Watergate, a controversial war, abandoned economic policies, a resignation, an assassination—no matter what the experiences of the past, the presidents say that this past can be disregarded. The problems will not continue because the presidency can make all things new.

3
Politics and Morality:
The Action

What this nation needs is an example from its elected
leaders in providing the spiritual and moral leadership
which no programs for material progress can satisfy.
—*Richard Nixon*

The major actors on the presidential stage are the president, the nation, and the American people. So one can ask what the presidents show themselves as doing, and what the nation and the American people do— what are said to be their appropriate roles. Does this activity vary with different philosophies of government or with distinct leadership styles? Does it change with the circumstances of the time or different agenda priorities? Alternatively, do presidents, whatever their circumstances, styles, or philosophies, present themselves in the same way? The addresses used in the preceding chapter can answer this additional range of questions.

Presidents and Political Activity

Winning Elections

A first answer is important although not surprising. Electoral activity is rarely mentioned in any of the addresses, whether inaugural, economic, or foreign policy. It could not be known from the presidents' accounts that they were associated with a party or had won an election. Indeed, one would not know how they had come to office, whether through election, monarchical succession, or divine anointing. While political references might not be expected in foreign policy speeches, they are very infrequent in inaugural and economic policy addresses as well.

Table 3.1 reports the number of references to parties or elections in inaugural and economic addresses. Any reference in the speech, not merely the subject of the sentence, is included: any mention of party or cognate forms, Republicans or Democrats, politics, elections, ballots, campaigns, or other synonyms. Where the word bipartisan is used alone as an adjective, the reference is not counted, although it should be noted that such references are rare.

Table 3.1
References to Elections and Parties in Inaugural and Economic Addresses[a]

	Inaugural Addresses		Economic Addresses		
	Number of Pages	Number of References	Number of Pages	Number of References	Combined References Every Two Pages
Truman	5.0	0	11.5	3	.4
Eisenhower	4.5	3	4.0	3	1.4
Kennedy	2.5	2	10.5	2	.6
Johnson	2.5	0	–	–[b]	.0
Nixon	3.5	0	19.0	13	1.2
Ford	2.0	10	22.0	7	1.4
Carter	2.5	0	5.0	1	.3
Reagan	4.0	0	32.5	34	1.9
Total	26.5	15	104.5	63	1.9

a. All words in the speech are counted referring to elections, campaigning, parties, or a political process. For details on the coding, see appendix B. Pages, taken from the *Public Papers*, are standardized to eliminate differences in type size. Partial pages are counted as one-half page.

b. No economic speeches were given in the time period.

While the inaugural follows the election, and in effect celebrates the election victory, presidents rarely refer to these events. An observer unfamiliar with American government would not know why presidents were there on the platform or how they had come to that position. The one exception, Ford's "Remarks on Taking Office," is explicitly not an inaugural address. Ford is willing to mention that he was not elected president:

> I am acutely aware that you have not elected me as your president by your ballots, and so I ask you to confirm me as your president with your prayers. . . .

After equating ballots and prayers as sources of legitimacy, he turns the situation to an advantage:

> If you have not chosen me by secret ballot, neither have I gained office by any secret promises. I have not campaigned either for the presidency or the vice presidency. I have not subscribed to any partisan platform.

Now this is amazing. The past party leader of the House of Representatives, and the Republican vice-president, has not subscribed to a partisan platform? Subscribing to a party platform is a bad thing for presidents to do? Advocates of stronger party government in the United States should be particularly interested in this. In any case, in almost the only reference found at an inaugural event, the president boasts that he is not identified with a political party. In the few other references to parties or elections, Eisenhower makes the general statement that "[our] faith decrees that we the people elect leaders not to rule but to serve," and Kennedy says that the inauguration is "not a victory of party but a celebration of freedom." Kennedy, like Ford, mentions parties only to deny their importance. The other presidents disassociate themselves completely from the idea and do not mention parties or elections at all.

The same pattern is found in the economic addresses. When parties are mentioned at all, they are used in two ways. First, they are modifiers of *congressional* activity: Presidents speak of the Democratic leadership, the majority party, Republicans and Democrats in the Congress. Second, they are referred to only to be denied: "It is not a question of party"; "not as Republicans or Democrats." Elections are a congressional activity, it appears from the presidential speeches. "It is an election year for Congress," Eisenhower remarks, the one time he mentions elections at all. Nixon repeats the point three times in his addresses. Congress evidently has parties, contests elections, and plays politics, all of which gets in the way, the presidents imply, of the public interest. No references to parties or elections are found in the foreign policy addresses, but none might be expected.

In all of the pages of inaugural and economic addresses, the parties or a synonym are mentioned only twenty times, with most of these references occurring in Reagan's April 1982 budget address. Even this speech, however, is less exceptional on a closer look. Reagan explains the stalemate on budget negotiations between the Democrats in Congress and his bipartisan Gang of 17, the former also referred to as the "Democratic side" and the latter as "our side." Calling the group the Gang of 17 carries on Reagan's characteristic informal style while allowing the Republican position to be cast in nonparty terms. Most party references in the speech are to the Democrats. Reagan is willing to make two statements on parties unique among the addresses: "There's no question but that a difference in philosophy exists" and "there hasn't been too much opportunity in the last 40 years to see what our philosophy can do." These straightforward descriptions of American party politics are the exceptions in presidential speech making. Nevertheless, it is clear that the president is attempting to distance himself from the party politics occurring in Congress. In most addresses presidents are so far removed from parties that they do not need to mention them.

The effect is capsulized in a reference by Nixon in a speech on 7 October 1971 to "many of my good friends in the field of politics." People might wonder what field Nixon was in when he fought Helen Gahagan

Douglas for a seat in the Senate, conducted the Alger Hiss investigation in Congress, and ran for vice-president. Or when he worked in the Eisenhower White House, campaigned for president in 1960 and again in 1968. Speaking as president, having successfully accomplished all of these various political activities, he disassociates himself from the field of his good friends.

The divorce between election and inauguration is quite a modern phenomenon in fact. The former twentieth century presidents, a later chapter will show, spoke of mandates, party platforms, and the verdict of the people. They not only explained what the election meant for the new administration coming to office, they acknowledged the tradition and obligation of doing so. It was a "tradition throughout our history," according to Herbert Hoover. An audience would know why these speakers were on the inaugural platform and what the celebration was about. It was the final step in the process of a democratic election. With the modern presidents this tradition is broken quite sharply and dramatically. The inauguration stands alone.

Whatever the modern presidents are doing, they are not engaging in such activity as winning elections or leading or speaking for their party. Congress engages in this activity (that is, when it is in session at all), but presidents do not. So, on election eve 1984, Reagan addresses the nation after a campaign of the highest professional caliber. He admits that he and George Bush have just finished traveling across the country:

> For me, a vivid recollection . . . will be from a whistletop train tour through Ohio in that historic car that once carried Franklin Roosevelt, Harry Truman, and Dwight Eisenhower across America. America had a smile in her heart that day. At each stop and through each community, whether gathered on their sidewalks, back lawns, or the plowed fields of their farms, again and again it was the young people I remembered— Cub Scouts in the blue shirts and bright yellow kerchiefs, high school bands, college crowds, and little girls perched atop their dads' shoulders. Well, they and a million more like them are what this election is all about.

Reagan is making another movie. Everything is vivid and bright. Politics is as scrubbed and clean as the Cub Scouts' kerchiefs and a modern election becomes a whistle-stop parade.

Persuading and Ordering

Other kinds of political activity call for reconciling group interests or forging compromises with Congress. But, as the preceding chapter suggests, such activity is rarely referred to, since other political actors rarely appear. Subnational groups are cast broadly to equal the American people; hence little conflict is suggested or reconciliation needed. Presidents do negotiate with other national leaders, as shown in the foreign policy addresses. Occasionally they say, too, in the economic addresses that they will meet the congressional leaders or that they have met with them. Much more frequently they simply ask, urge, or request Congress to act, with no direct consultation referred to. Overall, only 6 percent of verbs used with the presidential pronoun "I" refer to this activity. The point is seen more clearly in the following discussion.

Presidents are willing to show one kind of governmental activity they engage in—the giving of self-executing orders. Self-executing orders, as Neustadt describes them, are straightforward actions within the power of the executive that automatically produce results.[1] They need no persuasion or bargaining—that is, they need no political activity—to be carried out.

Neustadt cites such examples as Truman's firing of General Douglas MacArthur and Eisenhower's sending of federal troops to Little Rock. He emphasizes, however, that occasions for these self-executing orders are rare; hence the need to learn the power of persuasion. Despite the rareness of these activities, presidents appear willing to mention them when they occur. In foreign policy speeches they order, assign, direct, and announce decisions. In economic addresses they announce decisions, appoint special commissions, order federal pay postponements, name, and direct. In other words, presidents do show themselves using the powers of government; they are simply not willing to show why these powers have come to them or what is the source of legitimacy for their use.

An analysis of the main active verbs used in the speeches provides additional information. Table 3.2 reports the frequency of the predicates used with the subject "I" in all economic addresses to the nation given after the first year. All verbs in the active voice, omitting the verbs to be and to have and negatives, are counted. Of the three kinds of addresses studied, economic addresses can be considered the most political, in raising controversial issues and requiring compromise of different interests. Taking speeches after the first year, when the presidential honeymoon is over and when proposals have already been dealt with in Congress, highlights those occasions when we expect the most controversy and the greatest need for political action. Indeed, the speeches themselves are often given to rally the public in pushing Congress to pass administration proposals. Thus, by selecting the verbs used with the first-person singular, one can see what activity presidents say they engage in during these occasions.

Table 3.2
Presidential Activity as Described in Economic Addresses:
Main Verbs Used With the Pronoun "I"[a]

	References		
	Number	Number per Page	Percentage of All Verbs
Express thought/feelings	127	1.8	54
Make general statements/ take positions	67	1.0	29
Act/talk with others	41	0.6	17
Self-executing acts	(27)	(0.4)	(11)
Other specific acts	(14)	(0.2)	(6)
Total	235	3.4	100

a. All main verbs of active voice are counted with the exception of verbs "to be" and "to have" and negatives (e.g., "I will not delay"). Economic addresses following the first year include the following: Truman (14 June 1951); Eisenhower (15 March 1954); Kennedy (13 August 1962 and 18 September 1962); Nixon (17 June 1970, 15 August 1971, and 7 October 1971); Ford (24 March 1975, 13 January 1975, and 6 October 1975); and Reagan (4 April 1982, 16 August 1982, and 13 October 1982). The total number of speeches is 14 and the number of printed pages 69.5.

Activity is divided into three categories: expressing thought and feeling: making general statements and taking positions; and engaging in all other actions. These include self-executing orders and talking with others, whether to persuade, consult, or simply carry on communication. Verbs expressing thought and feeling include such words as *think, want, hope, believe, feel, know,* and appeals made directly to the American public as audience: "I say to you," "I call upon you," "I give [you] assurance." General statements simply express a sense of action without saying what the action will be: "I will do what I can," "I will do what I believe to be right," "I will take whatever steps are necessary," "I will use the powers of my office." Position taking asserts support or opposition for a particular proposal, but involves no other action beyond the assertion itself. It is typically used in relation to Congress, and with such verbs as *ask, propose, urge, insist, oppose, call on.* The final category, of all other actions, isolates specific activity that presidents describe themselves as taking.

Thinking and Feeling

Several points are immediately apparent from the results. First, since presidents do not use the first-person singular that frequently, references to their own actions are infrequent overall, averaging three sentences per printed page. A page, in other words, or the equivalent talking time, would not give that strong a sense of presidential activity. Second, expressions of thought and feeling are by far the most frequent activity expressed, constituting over half of the references, with general statements and positions ranking second, and specific activity third. Verbs expressing specific action constitute only 17 percent of the references overall, occurring about once every two pages. Finally, even when one does find a reference to specific activity, it tends to be a self-executing order. Self-executing actions outnumber all other specific actions at a rate of two to one. Any other activity, then, is rarely referred to: There are fourteen occasions altogether when such verbs are used, for an average of one every five pages.

Further information is provided by looking at the presidents separately. All the economic speeches tend to be the same length—from four to six printed pages. All presidents, except Nixon, use verbs most frequently to express thought or feeling, make general statements or take positions second most frequently, and describe other actions least frequently. Nixon uses general statements most frequently (25 times), expresses thought and feeling second in frequency (22 times), and describes a specific activity more frequently than the other presidents do (18 times). Indeed, Nixon is responsible for many of the self-executing orders reported in the table. In one speech he appoints a Cost of Living Council, directs the council, directs a secretary (twice), postpones federal pay raises, and orders a freeze. In another speech he appoints a commission (mentioned twice), appoints a Pay Board, and names an individual as director. In a third speech he relaxes a cutback, establishes a Pay Board, and instructs the Council of Economic Advisers to prepare a report. Since seventeen of the twenty-seven self-executing orders in table 3.2 are Nixon's, the frequency of specific actions reported would be even lower overall if the Nixon speeches were omitted.

More important, the fourteen other specific actions described in the table are also concentrated in a few addresses. Truman uses five in one speech. He calls in the congressional leaders and tells them things (twice). He says he is keeping after administration officials and has worked for the farmer. Reagan uses seven in the speech already referred to as exceptional in its willingness to mention political parties. He meets with his Gang of 17, receives reports, and tells them things. He asks his chief of staff to contact congressional leaders, meets with Republicans, and says he will consult with Democrats. He even says, "I called Speaker O'Neill." The notion of a president talking with the Speaker of the House is the only reference of its kind in all the economic speeches. For the remaining two cases, Nixon says he has consulted with representatives of labor and business, farmers and consumers, national, state, and local government officials; Ford says he will work with the Congress. All these activities are a standard part of the president's job of political persuasion, but they are rare exceptions in the economic addresses.

The action associated with the word "we" shows the same results and may be directly compared with table 3.2. Taking all main verbs used with the plural pronoun, the American people, and the nation, one finds only 10 percent describe specific actions as opposed to general statements or expressions of thought and feeling.[2] Most of the actions refer to particular accomplishments of the administration ("we have cut inflation by x percent"). Only five cases describe working or talking with others. Eisenhower says that we have asked Congress; Carter, that we have worked with Congress; Reagan, that we have worked with the cabinet, worked for a compromise budget, and agreed to limited revenue increases. These five cases are analogous to the fourteen in table 3.2.

Presidents show themselves at work in the following phrases: I believe, I only wish, I most earnestly hope, I think this is wrong. "I think it is imperative," Kennedy begins. "I agree with [George] Washington," Eisenhower points out. "I'm sure they did it with the best intentions," says Reagan. And Carter concludes: "I believe that our people . . . are equal to the task. I hope that you will prove me right." The activity of feeling is heightened by the frequency of other emotional words. The same speeches refer to misery, longing, tragedy, young couples struggling, only at our peril, and the terrible loss of another war. These quotations are all from economic addresses; emotions are even stronger in the inaugurals and some of the foreign policy speeches.

So, if one looks beyond parties and elections to other kinds of political activity, the result remains the same. Politics, even at the height of an economic controversy, is most noticeable by its absence. It is true of course that one action in a speech can speak louder than many feeling and thinking words. It is also true that the headlines will feature the one action—not all the other words. Nevertheless, if one asks about the kind of activity that presidents project, the result is clear and consistent. When any action is described, it is predominantly thinking and feeling, rarely specific, and only on the most exceptional occasions the kind that could be called political, in an attempt to talk with others or compromise different points of view.

An analysis by Lyn Ragsdale of the kinds of statements presidents make supplies additional information. Ragsdale distinguishes between statements of *policy action* (both promises and achievements), *policy discussion* (description of the national situation, facts, background), and *nonpolicy remarks*. She finds, consistent across presidents from Truman through Reagan, that policy discussion constitutes by far the largest share of the statements—62 percent of the statements overall, with action statements totaling 24 percent, and nonpolicy statements 14 percent. She concludes:

Interestingly, presidents make neither numerous policy promises, nor note a great many achievements being successfully carried out. And at times throughout their speeches, their remarks reflect no policy content at all. It appears that presidents pay particular attention to identifying and describing national problems. However, they are apparently much less likely to present plans of action designed to deal with the problems or announce specific actions actually taken regarding the problems.[3]

Self-executing orders would be coded within the policy action category, as would statements about meeting with congressional leaders. She adds that of course a single statement to end the war may be much more important than long paragraphs of background description. Nevertheless, the finding does stand in contrast to much of the conventional commentary about the need for vigor and energy in the office. Presidents appear to be talkers mainly—at least in their presentation to the American public—rather than doers.

A final point is important. All this avoidance of politics stands in direct contradiction to statements of political scientists about the office. In many ways, political scientists carry on the same symbolic emphasis that presidents do, but on the political dimension they take sharp exception. Writers on the presidency emphasize the electoral base as source of legitimacy, the president's position as party leader, and the need to strengthen the incumbent's political skill. Indeed, many writers suggest that one of the key weak points of the office is that its occupants have not been politically skillful enough. All writers stress the importance of elections as the fundamental link with the people and a source of power.[4] This is not to say, of course, that presidents do not know at least as well as the political scientists the importance of politics. Nevertheless, the portrayal of the office—as it is being shown to American citizens in their schools or before their television sets—is sharply different on this dimension.

Moral Leadership

If presidents do not engage in political activity, what do they do? Clearly, they engage in moral—and explicitly religious—activity. Literally they preach, reminding the American people of religious and moral principles and urging them to conduct themselves in accord with these principles. They lead prayers, quote from the Bible, and make theological statements about the Deity and His desires for the nation. We know from other studies that the public perceives presidents as altruistic and benevolent: They are the moral leaders and high priests of the American society.

This analysis suggests that presidents themselves are contributing to the impression and indeed consciously cultivating it.

Table 3.3 shows the frequency of religious and moral references in contrast to the political ones. Explicit religious references include biblical quotes, references to prayer or faith, religious imagery, or apocalyptic allusions. They do not include the broader references to morality that are kept separate in the table: words such as *moral, values, good, obligation, responsibility* (for details, see appendix B). Inaugurations, the table makes clear, are religious, not political, celebrations with references to God or other explicitly religious words as frequent as references to parties and elections are infrequent. The inaugural ratio of religious to partisan references is about 14 to 1. While religious references are fewer in the economic speeches, political references are also infrequent. Moral and religious words combined outweigh the political by a ratio of 2 to 1.

It is worth asking whether the ratio of religious to political references is changed by an election-year context. Inaugurals do not exist for the comparison, of course, nor are there enough economic addresses to compare for all presidents. It is possible, however, to compare State of the Union addresses in non-election years (the third year of the first full term) to those in the following, election year. The comparison shows no difference in results. If anything, the election years produce a slightly higher ratio of religious to political references. In 83 pages of nonelection-year addresses, one finds thirty explicit religious references and twelve political ones; in 75 pages of election-year addresses one finds thirty-five religious references and eleven political ones. State of the Union addresses appear less religious than the inaugurals, but more so than the economic policy speeches.[5]

A clearer sense of this religious leadership role can be gained from a reading of the inaugural speeches. Truman begins the 1949 inaugural asking for the help and prayers of the American people. He proclaims the essential principles of faith by which we live and calls our allies the millions who hunger and thirst after righteousness. Eisenhower begins with "a little private prayer" of his own, three paragraphs in length, and asks everyone to bow their heads. He says that we are governed by eternal moral and natural laws and speaks of the watchfulness of a Divine Providence. Johnson, like Eisenhower, is willing to name specific attributes of the Deity, pointing out that the judgment of God is harshest on those who are most favored. Carter uses two Bibles to take the presidential oath. Kennedy addresses the four clergymen who are present on the platform, invokes God twice in the first two paragraphs, quotes from Isaiah and paraphrases Romans (rejoicing in hope, patient in tribulation), and tells us that a good conscience is our only sure reward. He concludes by "asking His blessing and His help, but knowing that here on earth

Table 3.3

Religious, Moral, and Political Activity Compared: Number of References in Inaugural and Economic Addresses[a]

	Inaugural Addresses				Economic Addresses			
	N Pages	Religious	Moral	Political	N Pages	Religious	Moral	Political
Truman	5.0	12	9	0	11.5	5	12	3
Eisenhower	4.5	51	19	3	4.0	0	4	3
Kennedy	2.5	17	4	2	10.5	0	3	2
Johnson	2.5	19	5	0	—	—	—	—
Nixon	3.5	35	7	0	19.0	11	33	13
Ford	2.0	17	5	10	22.0	7	14	7
Carter	2.5	21	19	0	5.0	0	5	1
Reagan	4.0	24	12	0	32.5	10	39	34
Average references per 2 pages		14	6	1	per 3 pages	1	3	2

a. All words in the speech are counted wherever they appear. Partial pages are counted as one-half page, with pages standardized for differences of print in the *Public Papers*. Political references are taken from table 3.1.

God's work must truly be our own." That, in fact, is quite a secular statement for a presidential address. While Eisenhower and Ford give private prayers, Reagan urges a more public activity:

> I'm told that tens of thousands of prayer meetings are being held on this day and for that I'm deeply grateful. We are a nation under God, and I believe God intended for us to be free. It would be fitting and good, I think, if on each Inaugural Day in future years it should be declared a day of prayer.

This becomes the first proposal of the new administration.

Apocalyptic imagery is sounded in addresses from Truman through Nixon. Truman describes the international situation as a war between good and evil, lightness and dark, and Eisenhower sees the forces of good and evil massed and armed and opposed as rarely before in history. Kennedy says that a trumpet summons us in mankind's hour of maximum danger; Johnson prophesies that the hour and the day and the time are here; and Nixon announces the beginning of the third millennium. While this imagery is not found with the more recent presidents, the sermons continue. Carter tells us we must strengthen the American family, which is the basis of our society. Reagan says we must act worthy of ourselves, and Nixon gives an extended sermon on the crisis of the American spirit. The words would seem appropriate in any religious pulpit:

> Our crisis today is in reverse. We find ourselves rich in goods, but ragged in spirit. . . . To a crisis of the spirit, we need an answer of the spirit. And to find that answer, we need only look within ourselves. When we listen to "the better angels of our nature," we find that they celebrate the simple things, the basic things—such as goodness, decency, love, kindness.

He continues:

> In these difficult years, America has suffered from a fever of words; from inflated rhetoric that promises more than it can deliver; from angry rhetoric that fans discontents into hatreds; from bombastic rhetoric that postures instead of persuading. We cannot learn from one another until we stop shouting at one another—until we speak quietly enough so that our words can be heard as well as our voices.

Other moral references are found throughout the inaugural. Principles, virtues, and goodness are heard in almost every address. Decency, obligation, and duty are mentioned frequently. While the economic addresses, as might be expected, express fewer religious statements than the inaugurals, even here God is cited more frequently than the Council of Economic Advisers.

The moral words without religious meaning show a logic of their own. They are used so ambiguously that it is often impossible to determine the meaning in context. The ambiguity is often achieved by the repetition of a word in several senses. Thus *courage* in a moral sense shifts to a fighting courage and shifts again to the courage of economic entrepreneurs. *Principle* links moral tenets, political practices, and foreign policy positions. Reagan's heroes are not only soldiers killed in battle but ordinary citizens and families who pay taxes. Elsewhere, words that are not usually thought of as moral become so. Nixon calls for a braver and stronger America, implying a moral strength, and Reagan asks for a national renewal of strength and hope. The ambiguity is used so frequently as to seem deliberate. Like the plural pronoun seen in the previous chapter, the device links ideas of different meaning: The nation's history, goals, and economic system are painted with a common moral brush.

A ranking of the presidents as moral and religious leaders can be seen in table 3.4, based on the inaugural speeches. (Economic speeches could not be included since they vary greatly in length from one president to another. Thus the longer economic speeches added to the inaugurals would reduce the moral and religious emphasis for some presidents.) If one counts only the religious words in the inaugurals, Eisenhower and Nixon are the leaders with the plain-speaking Truman ranked lowest. Notice Carter's middle position. Many people thought his inaugural unique in its emphasis on religion, with two Bibles, a biblical quote, and the many moral and religious words. One writer called it a "revival

Table 3.4
The Moral and Religious Leaders[a]

	Pages	Number of References per Page Religious Words		Moral and Religious Words
Eisenhower	4.5	11	Eisenhower	16
Nixon	3.5	10	Carter	16
Ford	2.0	9	Nixon	12
Johnson	2.5	8	Ford	11
Carter	2.5	8	Johnson	10
Kennedy	2.5	7	Reagan	9
Reagan	4.0	6	Kennedy	8
Truman	5.0	2	Truman	4

a. Based on results from table 3.3, inaugural addresses only.

meeting."[6] But the born-again Christian was simply following the tradition of the office. Many presidents give *two* biblical quotes, one each from the Old and New Testament.

Carter, however, ranks highest in moral leadership; that is, in the use of moral words without religious meaning. Carter speaks of *principles, goodness, dignity, obligation,* and *responsibility. Moral* is used three times, *worthy* twice. Therefore, the combined ranking in the right-hand side of the table places Carter along with the three Republicans in the contest for the moral-religious title. Reagan remains with the Democratic presidents lower in the rankings, while Truman holds on to last place.

Reagan's ranking becomes clear by looking at the emphasis on economics in his inaugural, and the sad state of affairs that must be corrected by his years in office. This emphasis reduces the concentration of moral and religious ideas, although sections of his speech have as much religious emphasis as any of the presidents. God is mentioned five times, along with *prayer, faith, shrines, crosses, miracles,* and *sacrifice.* Nixon's position is also of interest. Symbolic statements need not be factually true, the introductory chapter pointed out. Thus it is perhaps not surprising that the president forced to resign after scandal and illegalities in office should also be a top-ranked moral and religious leader.

Beyond the party difference, with Republicans somewhat more likely to use religious references than Democrats, no other patterns appear. The earliest and the most recent presidents, as well as those elected on their own and those achieving office through succession, range from the bottom to the top of the ranking. No differences are found according to background religious faith. In the religious ranking a Catholic and a born-again Christian share a middle position while an Episcopalian and a Baptist rank lowest. It is true that several scholars have attempted to type the presidents according to the religious differences they bring to the White House. Fundamentalists might differ from traditional Christians or Calvinists from the Episcopalians.[7] This book suggests such an exercise would not be rewarding. The religious expression is an institutional, not an individual, component. When the speakers invoke God, call for sacrifice, or quote from the same biblical verses, they are speaking not as Catholics or Baptists, but as presidents. It is the similarity, not the difference, that requires people's attention. Overall, combining moral and religious words, one finds about ten references a page or, taking a page to equal about four minutes of speaking time, more than two references a minute. Clearly the expression of moral and religious ideas forms a dominant motif in this first speech on taking office.

Other evidence suggests that presidents believe in their role of moral leadership and take it seriously. A Kennedy adviser commented that "our presidents today have to be a personal model, a cultural articulator, and a semi-priest or semi-tribal leader. It will be less important in years to come for presidents to work out programs and serve as administrators than it will be for presidents . . . to serve as educational and psychic leaders." A Nixon aide wrote the following memorandum in 1967 to the would-be president:

> Potential presidents are measured against an ideal that's a combination of leading man, God, father, hero, pope, king. . . . They want him to be . . . someone to be held up to their children as a model; someone to be cherished by themselves as a revered member of the family, in somewhat the same way in which peasant families pray to the icon in the corner.

Carter was quoted in the National Journal to the effect that "the president is the only person who can speak with a clear voice to the American people and set a standard of ethics and morality, excellence and greatness."[8]

Dante Germino terms the American public philosophy "theocentric," or God-centered, pointing out that presidents since George Washington have emphasized God in their addresses.[9] The contemporary presidents are following this tradition. The tradition, of course, is part of a larger emphasis in American society: the civil religion or public philosophy that many writers have described. It is a nation "under God" according to its pledges, inscriptions, and currency. There are weekly prayer breakfasts held in the House and Senate too. Hence presidents are both responding to, and influencing, a larger set of expectations about government. Expected to be moral leaders for a moral nation, they energetically pursue the role. In doing so, they carry on the expectation for the next generation.

They do more than continue the tradition, however, a later chapter will show—they raise it to a new level. Comparing the modern presidents with their predecessors, one finds a difference both of degree and consistency. Some of the earlier presidents emphasized religion while others did not: there was no one agreed-on expectation. The pious Washington averaged eight religious references a page while Lincoln averaged less than one in his first inaugural address. All of the modern presidents except Truman rank higher than all of the earlier twentieth century presidents in their use of religious words and phrases. The former leaders, with five references per page, would place below Reagan in the first column of Table 3.4. The religious tradition has been heightened and institutionalized to become a major feature of the modern presidency.

Politics and Morality:
The Question of Boundaries

The surface activity does not tell the whole story. Political issues remain, recast as moral ones. A closer examination of the word *faith,* heavily used in all the addresses, can show the point more fully. Faith or a cognate form is used by all presidents except Ford in more than one meaning. Truman refers to faith in the Almighty and to the principles of faith by which we live. This latter faith, then, becomes democracy, which can be strengthened by Truman's economic recovery plan and North Atlantic treaty proposal. Eisenhower refers to political faiths as a euphemism for parties: faith of our fathers, faith in God, enemies of this faith (i.e., communist nations), faith, considered as trust, in freedom, and principle of faith, including a list of proposed foreign policy programs. The same word is given religious, patriotic, partisan, international, and legislative meanings. Johnson points out that American faith has brought victory in depression and war, linking religious faith with economic confidence. Reagan calls on the American people to renew their faith, singling out the entrepreneurs who have faith in themselves and in an idea and so create new jobs and new wealth.

Economic addresses show a similar blending of the moral and political. Kennedy urges us to fight for the American dollar and for freedom and Truman states that Congress must pass a strong anit-inflation law so the country can fight for world peace. In urging particular economic proposals Carter points out that "we enhance freedom in other lands by showing that our democratic system is worthy of emulation." Carter presumably is using democracy as a synonym for a capitalistic economy. Nixon calls for changes in the international exchange rates by observing that "a nation, like a person, has to have a certain inner drive in order to succeed. In economic affairs, that inner drive is called the competitive spirit." The American people must have faith in themselves if the nation is to stay number one in the world's economy. Therefore, the administration measures are designed "to help us snap out of the self-doubt, the self-disparagement that saps our energy and erodes our confidence in ourselves." Reagan points out that of two roads open for the American economy, only one will renew the American spirit. Cuts in government spending are cast in terms of Americans taking freedom back in their own hands. Thus support for the administration proposals becomes support for "our nationhood, our unrelenting fight for freedom, our very existence."

Just as the word "we" establishes equivalence between presidents, the American people, and the nation, so references to faith and moral strength establish another equivalence. They become devices for blending the moral so heavily emphasized with the political so vehemently denied. They thus add all the religious and moral fervor that has been invoked to support particular administration proposals.

However, morality is not used only to legitimize the political. It is one thing for presidents to elicit support by robing administration policies in religious terms. It is quite another to say that it is a good thing for American to pray (Reagan) or that they should hold the family unit together (Carter). With politics eliminated, the boundaries for presidential moral leadership become blurred to include both public and private activities. In other words, presidents do not limit their moral leadership to what some might call a public and political sphere. With the political suppressed, and Constitution transformed into "principles of faith," no guidelines remain to suggest limits to the moral activity.

Two examples can take the point further. Nixon's inaugural goes to some length in describing a crisis of the American spirit. There is discord, division, and empty lives seeking fulfillment. There are tasks that need doing that wait for hands to do them. For this moral crisis the president offers a moral solution. The better angels of our nature say (1) that the American people should lower their voices; (2) that they should look to simpler things because greatness comes in simple trappings; and (3) that the most important enterprises are not grand but "those small, splendid efforts that make headlines in the neighborhood newspaper instead of the national journal." These are actually quite extreme political statements. The president of the United States is saying that citizens should not be so concerned about national affairs, that they should not debate issues—say, the war in Vietnam—but it would be morally better for them to concentrate on neighborhood affairs.

Reagan makes a similar point, although less obviously, in his inaugural when he praises volunteerism and community pride and speaks of the heroes of everyday life:

> Those who say that we're in a time when there are no heroes, they just don't know where to look. You can see heroes every day going in and out of factory gates. . . . You meet heroes across a counter. And they're on both sides of that counter. . . . They're individuals and families whose taxes support the government. . . . Their patriotism is quiet but deep.

The meaning of *hero*, that of a person of extraordinary traits or achievement, has been turned into its opposite and given the president's praise. Reagan's heroes, like the people who listened to Nixon's angels, would mind their own business, be quiet, and concentrate their energies on community matters.

Neither statement says that citizens should not speak, assemble, or petition on national affairs. Both statements, however, strongly suggest that it would be morally better and more praiseworthy to do other things. They challenge a political idea, of the role of citizens in a democratic government, by claiming a moral authority on the part of presidents. If the moral authority is taken as legitimate, in these or any other statements, then these political traditions must be subject to question.

At present, this moral authority is used in at least three different ways. It is used to argue for specific proposals: for example, inflation controls to bring world peace. It is used to offer a president's personal opinion on other subjects: prayer, the family, abortion. And it is used to enunciate broad political positions that challenge other political traditions: Citizens should lower their voices and reduce dissent. No one, least of all the presidents, has asked whether all or any of these uses is appropriate to the office.

The Moral Nation

The American people too are moral, we see in the addresses. They are idealistic and self-sacrificing. They hold to principles of religious and democratic faith, they have faith in themselves, and they show the competitive spirit that has made the nation great. But the people's primary moral role, according to the presidents, is to support the economy. Morality is tested and demonstrated in economic terms. Truman's logic is straightforward:

> If inflation gets away from us . . . it would be the easiest victory the Kremlin could ask for . . . [therefore] when some of us have to take a cut in profits, or pass up a wage increase we might otherwise get, let us remember that we are making a contribution to the peace of the world.

Truman speaks of sacrifice; Kennedy, responsibility; Nixon, a strong and healthy spirit. Nixon explains that the "good life is the active, productive, working life—the life that gives as well as gets." Reagan talks of stamina and faith, and Ford of self-discipline and the will to win. Each is presenting a policy for inflation controls. The speeches follow a two-step pattern in which presidents tell the nation what is moral and then assert their confidence that Americans will do the moral thing. Since citizens of the past had the moral strength to found the nation, make it great, and sacrifice in wars, the present body of citizens should have this strength too. Truman mentions the men fighting in Korea. Ford and Carter remind people of World War II.

Above all, the nation is a moral actor, embodying the highest virtues and noblest aims. Three major themes are emphasized in inaugural, economic, and foreign policy speeches from the 1940s to the 1980s and through all the events of American history that took place in that time.

First, as other writers point out, the nation is moral because it works for the noblest goals: It seeks to bring peace and freedom to the world. The nation itself symbolizes freedom, from its beginnings and war for independence. But it also, altruistically, will work for freedom elsewhere and for peace. Germino documents how the national mission has been transformed in recent administrations to international activism: The nation not only represents freedom in the world but will actively lead other nations to this goal.[11] *Like the president, the nation is a moral leader.* Truman tells us that other nations look to the United States for peace and freedom. Eisenhower says that destiny has laid upon our country the responsibility of the free world's leadership. Kennedy calls the nation the leader of the free world in its fight against tyranny, poverty, disease, and war. Nixon sees the nation as a peacemaker: It will lead the world to peace and make the world safe for mankind. And Reagan describes the nation as a beacon of hope for those who do not have freedom.

The same theme is repeated in the economic and foreign policy speeches. Truman's anti-inflation program is necessary to fight for world peace. A Kennedy proposal is critical for the well-being of the countries that so greatly depend on us, while an economic aid program can convince other countries of the advantages of freedom. Nixon's tariff and exchange-rate policy can strengthen the country in order to work for peace and freedom in the world, and, according to Reagan, the marines were sent to Lebanon to "serve the cause of world peace and the future of mankind."

Second, the nation is moral because of its association with God. Its mission of freedom, however defined, is either given directly by God or has at least received divine blessing. Nixon associates the nation's destiny with the will of God. Kennedy implies that what the nation does on earth will be God's work. And Truman says, "I believe . . . Almighty God has set before this nation the greatest task in the history of mankind." Johnson says merely that the nation has been "allowed by God to seek greatness through its own work and spiritual strength." According to Germino, in the American public philosophy as expressed by presidents throughout American history, "God has made of America his chosen country."[12] And James Robertson summarizes the point:

> The mission and the destiny were inherent in the Revolution: democratic government, equality, and individual pursuit of happiness were the legitimate inheritance of all mankind . . . and Americans were charged by God (as His chosen people) to represent all mankind and to bring the blessings of His inheritance to the world.[13]

The nation is moral because of its connection with the larger divine purpose.

Third, the nation is moral because it seeks no territory or personal aggrandizement as it pursues its world mission. It is altruistic and innocent of selfish ends.[14] The point is repeated so frequently in all addresses as to seem obligatory:

> We seek no territory . . .
> We have sought no territory. We have imposed our will on no one . . .
> We seek no dominion over our fellow man, but man's dominion over tyranny and misery . . .
> We do not seek to intimidate. . . .

Truman's 15 December 1950 speech to the nation initiating action in Korea was accompanied by the following words:

> We have no aggressive purpose. We will not use our strength for aggression. We are a tolerant and restrained people, deeply aware of our moral responsibilities and deeply aware of the horrors of war.

Johnson says on 29 September 1967:

> The true peace-keepers are those men who stand out there . . . at this very hour, taking the worst that the enemy can give. The true peace-keepers are the soldiers who are breaking the terrorist's grip around the villages of Vietnam. . . .

The true peace-keepers are soldiers. Johnson accompanies his announcement of action in the Dominican Republic by saying that the nation does not seek to interfere with other countries or influence their choice of governments. And on 20 September 1982 Reagan explains that he sent the marines to Lebanon "for peace in the Mid-East and a safer world. . . . Both our purposes and our actions are peaceful." As Eisenhower summarizes, "We fight wars for peace."

In a very perceptive essay William Blanchard analyzes the American attitude toward war. "It is apparent," he says, "that the American president and many other leading public officials have a strong belief in their own good intentions and in their capacity for altruism." While they often seek to expand American power, they must not do so deliberately or aggressively. Hence they use some event, either real or manufactured, as a pretext for action:

> Although we are restrained in our desire for achievement by the thought that we must not take from others, must not be bullies, we can

strike all the more forcefully if we are provoked, that is, if we can believe that the other fellow started it. . . . The very fact that the other person strikes first releases us from all restraint. He becomes a "bad" person (or nation), and it becomes acceptable for us to punish him. That is why our foreign policy appears to be reactive.[15]

Blanchard is speaking of American foreign policy throughout the twentieth century. The insistence, then, among the contemporary presidents that Americans "fight wars for peace" is part of a larger and deeper national tradition. In Germino's term it is part of the American public philosophy that presidents both believe in and seek to express.

Following the algebraic logic of the symbolism, things equal to the same thing are equal to each other. Thus, as the people and the nation are characterized by high moral standards, so is the president. As the nation is strong and is looked to for leadership, so is the president. Both the nation and the president are moral leaders. The equivalence of actors is therefore reinforced and extended by the equivalence of action, as shown in figure 3.1. By emphasizing moral activity, presidents first of all strengthen the identification of themselves with the nation; second, they justify specific political activity, without naming it as political; and finally,

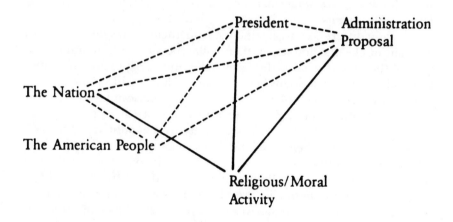

------Equivalence established by word "we"

———Association with religious/moral activity

Figure 3.1
The Actors and Their Activity

they rally support for the administration by invoking patriotic and religious feelings. If the point of the speech is to call forth support for the president and administration programs (the upper right-hand portion of the diagram), then a powerful emotional arsenal indeed is mobilized for this effect.

Summary

The activity presented in the major addresses shows a consistency across presidents independent of differences in personality, political background, and rhetorical style. All shun parties and elections, whatever their personal enjoyment of politics or experience as past party leader (Johnson, Ford), career politician (Kennedy, Nixon), or relative newcomer to the national political scene (Eisenhower, Carter).[16] All emphasize the expression of thought and feeling and say little about specific actions taken. Nixon's use of self-executing orders, while unusual, does not change the overall similarity. Indeed, if presidents are expected to be active and energetic in their years in the White House, they give scant sense of this energy in the verbs used in the major speeches. All of the presidents emphasize religion and morality independently of their own beliefs or their parties' on the role of religion in government, although the Republicans are somewhat more likely to use religious references than the Democrats.

The slight differences are intriguing. Nonetheless, presidents are more like than unlike one another in their willingness to act as moral leaders and tell the people what is the Divine Will in regard to administration proposals. Reagan was identified with a constituency in the Republican party concerned with emphasizing religion in American life and returning prayer to the schools. Yet, Reagan was no more likely to emphasize his role as religious leader, at least as measured quantitatively in these addresses, than the other presidents. This is not to say that backgrounds and ideologies would not affect decisions on religious issues or the role of religion in government. Rather, in terms of the picture of the office being presented to the public, presidents show a striking consistency.

Some of this consistency derives from the larger American tradition where the nation is associated with God from its beginnings and where party politics has negative connotations. To some extent, presidents are merely expressing what they believe the public wants to hear. Presidents throughout American history have shunned parties and envisioned a moral mission for the nation, whether in national or international terms. While the particular mission varies, as each president casts it anew, it is essentially the same, connecting the nation with the cause of freedom and divine blessing. Thus, Calvin Coolidge explains in his inaugural address of 1925:

> America seeks no earthly empire built on blood or force. No ambition, no temptation, lures her to thought of foreign dominations. The legions which she sends forth are armed, not with the sword, but with the cross. The higher state to which she seeks the allegiance of all mankind is not of human, but of divine origin. She cherishes no purpose save to merit the favor of Almighty God.

In a clear similarity to the modern presidents, Coolidge asserts that the nation seeks no empire or foreign domination and that U.S. foreign policy carries out a divine purpose. Four of the five sentences quoted make explicit religious references, with the fifth, in seeking "no earthly empire," implying the idea that a heavenly empire is sought. Contemporary speakers might not use the imagery of the Christian soldiers marching under the banner of the cross, but the effect is the same. Coolidge, a president not known for his rousing rhetoric, calls on the nation—as Truman, Kennedy, and Nixon will call later—to do God's work.

This does not mean that the role of moral leaders is fixed or static. One writer sees a rise of religion in the White House occurring through the Carter and Reagan years. Carter, he argues, was more willing to make his religion public, and Reagan was more explicit in his ties to religious groups.[17] If presidents can preach, then preachers can run for president as Jesse Jackson and Pat Robertson made clear. Morality and emotional fervor become issues in presidential campaigns. Article 2 of the Constitution leaves the office sufficiently undefined, as to be open to interpretation. So, to the extent that journalists, the public, and the presidents themselves accept and seek to expand this moral leadership role, the office will change accordingly.

What is emerging, then, is a clearer sense of the institution of the presidency, existing independently of individual occupants or the circumstances of the time. Presentation of the office in a very real sense becomes the office: It is what people present it to be. So, to the extent that presidents are contributing to this definition, the findings of the chapter are important. Presidents say they are moral, not political, leaders. They do not negotiate with Congress or win elections or engage in much specific activity at all. Instead, they believe and feel things. They take positions and tell the American people what is good, whether in public or private life. At the same time, another historical tradition— concerning the lines that should be drawn between church and state—is not being carried on in the institution.

Presidents should think and feel and not play politics. These are the job descriptions heard from all the presidential pulpits. However, candidates elected only for their thinking and feeling, or their appearance of doing so, may not be able to govern. Jimmy Carter was criticized for his failure to translate some very noble goals into political reality.[18] Carter, according to one biographer, was a problem solver, who sought out policies of the public good, bending his energies to solve these problems and letting the political consequences follow.[19] The consequences confounded many of the Carter administration goals. Carter was not an isolated example, as the 1988 election campaign showed. Two ministers ran for president. Debates were scored as to which candidate showed more passion than the other. According to the symbolic presidency, this was a key requirement of the job. Political skill need not conflict with passion or moral purpose, and yet political leaders face heavy disadvantages in the modern election campaign. Their own skills cannot be talked about, while the semblance of passion and the role of moral leader are more highly polished by those of other professions.

A final point, implicitly throughout the chapter, deserves restating. The American public, both children and adults, see the president as benevolent and altruistic, representing and speaking for the morality of the nation. Many presidential scholars emphasize the same morality in works from the 1940s through the 1980s. One finds, then, the hypothesized convergence between presidents and others in emphasizing this moral role. The one qualification is that presidents are even more consistent than others in this emphasis. In sharp contrast to the politics of the selection process or the complexity of governing a modern secular state, the reality is presented simply as a problem of moral leadership. The nation and its chief representative are recast along lines that people would like to believe are true.

4

The Burden of the Office:
The Audience

I will be the President of black, brown, red, and white
Americans, of old and young, of women's liberationists
and male chauvinists and all the rest of us in-between, of
the poor and the rich, of native sons and new refugees, of
those who work at lathes or at desks or in mines or in the
fields, of Christians, Jews, Moslems, Buddhists, and
atheists, if there really are any atheists after what we
have all been through.—*Gerald Ford*

The national addresses analyzed thus far constitute a small part of the
total activity. Presidents present themselves much more frequently and
more regularly in addresses to smaller groups of Americans. As one
writer describes it,

> The White House is flooded by requests for personal appearances or
> messages for national conventions, ground-breaking ceremonies, fund
> raisers and testimonials. Groups and delegations seek audiences to
> lobby for pet projects or simply to bask in the presidential aura. All
> presidents, reportedly even George Washington, have had to make
> provisions for responding to such entreaties.[1]

According to one Eisenhower aide, these are "the Pastoral Duties of the
President encountered in shepherding his far-flung flock." Presidents
shuttle from Maine to Salt Lake City and back to the obligatory groups
in the Rose Garden. Armies of staff workers coordinate each step along
the way. In the first thousand days in office, presidents since Kennedy
average nearly one scheduled address each working day. Adding travel
time, one writer estimates that Nixon and Carter spent one third of their
first three years in office on these appearances.[2]

Who do the presidents talk to in all this time-consuming activity? How
do the minor addresses alter or extend the pictures of government found
in the major speeches? This chapter looks at the range of activity presidents engage in and the kind of audience addressed. It then asks to what
extent the particular audience changes the presidential presentations. A
minor address is taken as a speech actually delivered by the president of
more than one page of words, as listed in the *Public Papers,* and addressed
to a specific audience and not to Congress or the American people as a
whole. Telephone messages and indirect transmissions, as well as ex-

changes such as interviews, question-and-answer sessions, and joint remarks, are excluded. Minor addresses can be made in the White House
or elsewhere in Washington or at any points throughout the United
States and abroad.

The minor addresses, shown in the first row of table 4.1, can be seen
in the context of other messages. No increase occurs since the Kennedy
years in the number of minor addresses delivered or in the total of minor
addresses plus briefer remarks. After the Eisenhower years, the total
number of remarks increases for all presidents, but does not increase
further across time. The number of exchanges varies with individual
presidents, with Truman and Eisenhower holding more news conferences than the more recent presidents do, and Kennedy and Carter
scheduling more joint remarks with visiting foreign dignitaries.[3]

These results differ from a study by William Lammers that suggests
minor addresses have been steadily increasing. Lammers excludes
speeches given in the White House, on the grounds, or in the Executive
Office Building. Thus, remarks to local officials in Des Moines would be
included, while remarks to the Boy Scouts or foreign dignitaries in the
White House would not be included.[4] The Lammers study highlights
physical activity as required for travel rather than verbal or speechmaking activity per se. Presidential travel has increased, with the increase
in air speed and efficiency; hence the speeches outside Washington have
increased. The total number of minor addresses, however, has not
changed substantially since the Kennedy years.

Table 4.1
Minor Addresses, Remarks, and Exchanges, Truman to Reagan[a]

| | Number of Cases | | | | | | | | |
	T	E	K	J	N	F	C	R	Total
Minor addresses	120	150	176	428	308	285	362	347	2176
Brief remarks	148	67	430	241	239	148	231	280	1784
Total	268	217	606	669	547	433	593	627	3960
Exchanges	153	126	430	179	137	155	325	286	1791
Total N	421	343	1036	848	684	588	918	913	5751

a. Minor addresses are remarks delivered in person by presidents; brief remarks are
those of one page or less. Exchanges include all remarks delivered in conjunction with
others: news conferences, question-and-answer sessions, toasts, and joint statements with
foreign dignitaries. The remaining entries in the *Public Papers* are written and transcribed
messages, by telephone, tape, or other indirect transmission. Radio addresses are included
only for the Truman administration; hence, Reagan's regular radio broadcasts would add
82 cases to his total. All cases in the first three years of each term are included; Ford's are
listed for his partial term.

Presidential Audiences

The range and variety of minor addresses can be seen in tables 4.2. The classification used in the tables gives a first sense of the breadth of presidential activity. It also distinguishes the various kinds: the *governmental,* including remarks on the national government and international affairs; as distinguished from the *political,* including remarks to party groups, economic interest groups, and regional ceremonies; and distinguished from the *cultural-ceremonial,* including remarks at all ceremonies and speeches to cultural and religious groups. All these activities are "political" in the sense that presidents find them useful in maintaining public support. Nevertheless, to investigate how presidents spend their time and what picture of themselves they present, the distinctions are important. In major addresses, as earlier chapters made clear, presidents make few references to actual government activity, speaking instead of their hopes and beliefs for the nation and equating themselves with national and patriotic symbols. In the role of moral leader, they emphasize the cultural and religious more than the political, shunning refer-

Table 4.2
Classification of Minor Addresses by Audience and Subject, Truman to Reagan[a]

	Percentage of Addresses								
	T	E	K	J	N	F	C	R	Total
National government	5	0	7	27	17	14	19	11	15
International affairs	6	5	27	16	15	8	11	12	14
Party groups	13	14	6	3	4	15	16	16	11
Economic interest groups	8	21	13	10	11	13	15	19	13
Regional travel—general	25	19	24	8	19	17	7	7	14
Religious/cultural groups	20	26	16	18	17	16	18	23	19
Ceremonial affairs	20	13	6	15	16	15	12	12	14
Other	3	2	1	2	0	1	1	1	1
Total minor addresses %	100	100	100	99	99	99	99	100	101
N	120	150	176	428	308	285	362	347	2176

	Summary Classification of Minor Addresses[b]								
	T	E	K	J	N	F	C	R	Total
Governmental affairs	11	5	34	43	32	22	30	23	29
Party/groups/region	46	54	43	21	34	45	38	42	38
Religious/cultural/ceremonial	40	39	22	33	33	31	30	35	33

a. Based on the first row of table 4.1: addresses in the first three years of the term that total more than one page in the *Public Papers.* Percentages may not sum to 100 due to rounding. For details on the classification scheme, see appendix C.

b. Based on the results of table 4.2, excludes the addresses classified as "other."

ences to parties and economic interest groups. To what extent, then, is a similar or different impression created by the minor addresses? What do the presidents do?

As leaders of all the people, the presidents distribute their time widely across a range of different audiences. Governmental addresses constitute less than one-third of the minor speeches delivered, and considerably less than one-third for Truman, Eisenhower, Ford, and Reagan. These addresses include all remarks on signing bills and making appointments and nominations; all remarks to Congress; government agencies, or other national government personnel; any remarks on specific government policies; all remarks to representatives of foreign nations, whether here or abroad; and all remarks to international organizations. Political addresses constitute a slightly larger category, represented by 38 percent of the addresses overall. This leaves one-third of the addresses devoted to ceremonial and religious and cultural affairs, and considerably more than one-third if the regional ceremonies were included. For all presidents except Kennedy, the addresses to religious and cultural groups constitute the largest or second-largest category in the table.

Overall, the impression created by the minor addresses supports the results from previous chapters. One finds the same attention to religious and cultural matters and a deemphasis on party affairs. The ceremonial functions of office (the second-to-the-last row in table 4.2) form as prominent a part of the schedule as the national government functions (the first row in the table). Speeches to religious and cultural groups outnumber those to party or economic interest groups. While party speeches have increased for the three most recent presidents—Ford, Carter, and Reagan—these speeches remain the least frequent of the activities listed in table 4.2

A clear difference, however, from earlier results is also apparent. In contrast to the similarity of the major addresses, presidents vary greatly in the audiences selected for minor speeches. See Kennedy's unique emphasis on international affairs and Johnson's on national government, primarily occasions of signing bills into law. Nixon addresses nearly every government agency and department for his share of national government activity and makes few speeches concerning legislation. Reagan pays more attention to economic groups than his predecessors did. Ford and Eisenhower give relatively less attention to speeches on national and international affairs.

Presidents appear to be following their own agendas in the audiences they choose to address. In fact, the speeches provide a good shorthand record for some of the characteristic features of each administration. With Kennedy, the White House becomes cosmopolitan, a center and gathering place for visits of foreign dignitaries. Johnson builds his Great

Society program, with a speech and a White House ceremony for each bill that becomes law. Nixon ignores an uncooperative Congress, pushing domestic programs by working within the executive branch. Many of Reagan's economic group speeches are to Hispanic Americans, setting forth his policy on Nicaragua. There are seven speeches to Hispanic groups in 1983 alone. Nearly half of his international speeches also address Latin American subjects.

Presidents follow their own agenda in the timing of speeches too. Nixon schedules the most speeches in his first year, Kennedy in his third, and Truman divides his evenly across the years. The other presidents schedule the second year most heavily. Johnson packs his schedule in the first three months of 1965, while Reagan and Kennedy schedule very few minor addresses in their first three months in office. Kennedy does schedule meetings with Protestant and Jewish groups in the early weeks, perhaps to reassure people about the first Catholic president. Party speeches are scheduled most heavily by Truman and Nixon in their first year, Johnson in his third, and the other presidents in their second year. One might expect to find the greatest number of minor addresses in the second year, after the first legislation is under way and before the mid-term congressional elections. Although the second year is favored overall in the scheduling of these speeches, there is great variation.

The differences carry also to the particular groups addressed within the category. Republicans Eisenhower and Ford speak frequently to business groups and rarely to labor; Nixon, Reagan, and Democrats Kennedy, Johnson, and Carter speak to both groups. Kennedy, in fact, balances his talks within the week: in the week of 6 December 1961 speaking to the National Association of Manufacturers and the American Federation of Labor, at the end of April 1962 addressing a chamber of commerce and the United Auto Workers, and on 18 November 1963 speaking to the United Steelworkers and a chamber of commerce. Truman, in contrast, addresses no labor or business groups. Johnson and Carter speak frequently to minority groups and women, whereas the other presidents do not. The minority groups addressed by Johnson do not continue to receive addresses in the Nixon administration, nor do Carter's speeches to blacks and women carry on to the Reagan years.

Straight numerical comparisons can be misleading, however. The White House is ingenious in combining characteristics—to get two groups, as it were, for the price of one. So, speeches are scheduled with black clergymen, black musicians, and women working for civil defense. Reagan addresses four black groups in his first three years in office: the NAACP, the Black Republican Council, representatives of black colleges and universities, and the National Council of Negro Women. To this last group, he tells the story of how his father would not let him see *The Birth of a Nation* because of its racist scenes. He also tells them about a black friend he used to play football with. Carter's eight speeches to black groups—twice to the Congressional Black Caucus—are not directly comparable.

A look at business groups provides another illustration. All presidents speak more frequently to business than labor: Carter's and Reagan's ratio is about 3 to 1. Both presidents speak to small business groups and find ways to combine groups, addressing black and women business executives and a Hispanic chamber of commerce. But unlike Carter, Reagan speaks twice to the National Association of Manufacturers and addresses two national realtor groups. He meets four times with CEOs of large organizations. While the ratio is similar, perhaps reflecting the number and diversity of business groups, it is possible to separate the Democrat from the Republican in these speeches.

The cultural-religious groups show the presidents at work in their moral leadership role. Truman addresses the Masons four times, the Presbyterians, a Pilgrimage of American Churchmen, and the National Conference of Christians and Jews. Eisenhower addresses the Masons, the National Council of Churches, the Conference of United Church Women, the World Christian Endeavor Convention, the World Council of Churches, a B'nai B'rith dinner, the American Jewish Tercentary Dinner, and the National Council of Catholic Women. Presidents after Eisenhower give fewer talks proportionately to religious groups, adding remarks to groups in sports, science, and the arts. Kennedy addresses the Mormons, a Protestant Council, and an International Christian Leadership group, but he also speaks at a National Football Hall of Fame banquet and gatherings at the National Academy of Sciences and the National Gallery of Art. Johnson speaks to the Methodists twice, the Council of National Fraternal Organizations, and a Jewish Labor Committee Dinner; but he adds Girls Nation to the traditional Boy Scout address, speaks on three occasions to youth groups interested in science, and gives speeches honoring football players, physical fitness, teaching, the Encyclopedia Britannica, and the Council for the Creative and Performing Arts. Nixon speaks at a church service in Honolulu, addresses American priests at the Vatican, delivers remarks on meeting the pope, and gives several speeches at ceremonies for Billy Graham. He also addresses the Knights of Columbus, the Junior League, football groups (four times), the Associated Council of the Arts, and the Bob Hope Christmas Show. Ford addresses the Baptists, the Lutherans, and the Society of Religious Broadcasters, as well as sports groups (football, golf, yacht racing, college athletics), high school students, Boys Nation, the Boy Scouts, and the YMCA. All presidents speak at the annual presidential prayer breakfasts, give a Christmas message to

Americans, and make a speech at the lighting of the White House Christmas tree.

Carter emphasizes religion more than his Democratic predecessors did. He gives remarks at a Chanukah ceremony in addition to the traditional Christmas addresses and gives a speech at a Day of Remembrance for Victims of the Holocaust. He also speaks to the Southern Baptists twice, the National Conference of Christians and Jews, the Mormons, the Conference on Religion and Peace, and makes an address on meeting the pope. Reagan continues the religious emphasis, adding speeches to evangelicals and religious broadcasters and attending several ceremonies of prayer. He addresses many Jewish groups, one Catholic group, and no Protestants other than the evangelicals.

The presidents' favorite groups, measured as those receiving the most addresses in the first three years, are listed below:

Truman	Masons
Eisenhower	Religious groups
Kennedy	Youth groups
Johnson	Colleges
Nixon	Religious groups
Ford	Sports
Carter	Religious groups
Reagan	Religious groups

While there are signs of a broadening of the cultural role beyond traditional religious groups, it is not a secularization. That is, the religious ceremonies remain across the time period along with the more secular addresses. The point can be seen more clearly by looking at the Republican presidents spanning three decades: Eisenhower, Nixon, and Reagan. Eisenhower's addresses are primarily to religious and youth and education groups, with no sports, arts, or scientific groups addressed. By the Nixon administration, all these groups are represented in the speeches: religious groups, 16 times; youth and education groups, 17; arts, science, and medicine, 12; and sports, 6, along with miscellaneous others. By the Reagan administration all these groups are addressed, with the addition of a number of speeches to family and community service groups along with others: religious groups, 14 times; youth and education, 21; arts, science, and medicine, 15; and sports, 6. As the groups themselves have increased through the 1980s, presidents struggle to keep pace in their minor addresses.

So, today, presidents still preside at national prayer breakfasts, address a Catholic Education Association, the Anti-Defamation League, and the Association of Evangelicals. They also give medals for excellence in education, science, physical fitness, community service, and youthful bravery. They propose new "Academic Fitness Awards," and give a Presidential

Medal of Freedom to western writer Louis L'Amour. In addition, they address groups in mental health, arts and humanities, vocational training, and crime fighting. They preside at a National Family Week celebration and visit the hockey All Stars, the NBA champions, a health fair, a medical conference, and Disney World.

The expansion of this religious-cultural role is shown dramatically in table 4.3. Increasingly, presidents speak with authority on matters of art, education, science, medicine, and family life. Just as they are willing to explain why the Deity favors a particular Latin American policy, so they enunciate standards of personal achievement and canons of education. Johnson gives his observations on the state of creative and performing arts in America, and Reagan explains his philosophy of education. In a speech on 8 December 1983, Reagan speaks to the National Forum on Excellence in Education. Although he warns that academic standards should not be set by the government in Washington, he goes on to say what these standards should be. American schools, according to the president of the United States, do not need vast new sums of money as much as they need fundamental reforms. They should "restore good, old-fashioned discipline," "teach the basics," and teach values about religion and family life. A Presidential Commission on Academic Fitness will define these standards and give academic fitness awards.

Presidents are clearly picking their own audiences in these addresses and transmitting a sense of personal style in the process. Clearly, also,

Table 4.3
Growth of the President's Role as Religious and Cultural Leader

Groups Addressed	T	E	K	J	N	F	C	R
Religion	x	x	x	x	x	x	x	x
Fraternal groups	x	x	x	x	x	x	x	x
Journalism	x	x	x	x	x	x	x	x
Youth	x	x	x	x	x	x	x	x
Education	x	x	x	x	x	x	x	x
Science	x		x	x	x	x	x	x
Medicine			x	x	x	x	x	x
Arts			x	x	x	x	x	x
Sports			x	x	x	x	x	x
Physical fitness			x	x	x	x	x	x
Entertainment					x	x	x	x
Mental health							x	x
Community service							x	x
The family							x	x

Note: An "x" indicates at least one speech to the group in the first three years. In other miscellaneous cases, Kennedy also addressed the Sponsors and Editors of Historical Publications, and Carter spoke to an association of librarians.

some groups enjoy more access to the White House than others, and this access varies from one president to another. While all presidents now maintain liaison staff with groups such as blacks, women, and the elderly, they vary in the attention they give these groups.[5] The schedule is in fact a political scorecard, reflecting which groups have succeeded in gaining White House access and which are important to presidents in maintaining their coalitions and building new support. See Kennedy's care in addressing Protestant and Jewish groups in his first weeks in office and Reagan's targeting of Hispanic groups.

These results follow closely another measure of group representation available for the Carter and Reagan years.[6] These are the first presidents to print the official schedule in the *Public Papers,* including their private meetings with various groups. A public address to the groups would be included in the schedule, but so would a closed meeting with the group representatives. According to this fuller measure, Carter and Reagan are alike in the number of meetings they schedule and the range of groups they speak with: business, labor, farming, culture, religion, minorities, and others. They are unalike, however, in the particular groups they meet with most frequently. Carter's leading groups are cultural-religious, unions, and business, in that order, while Reagan's are business, cultural-religious, and conservatives. To judge by the schedule, both presidents meet frequently with minorities: about once every three weeks through the first three years of the term. Nevertheless, Carter meets with black groups twice as often as Reagan does. Nearly half (42) percent) of Reagan's meeting with minorities are with Hispanic groups.

Nevertheless, the overall impression from the minor speeches extends the previous findings in several important ways. First, one finds the same down-playing of the political activity concerning parties and interest groups. The major addresses give no indication of a conflict among interest groups. The minor addresses carry on this impression. Any hint of conflict, as between business and labor groups, is either ignored by Truman, balanced by Kennedy, or engulfed by Johnson in the many other audiences addressed. Only rarely could one say that a president appears associated with particular interest groups. This is the president of all the people, the young and the old, the rich and the poor, the black and the white. Just as the major speeches combine groups to add up to the American people, so the schedule of minor addresses gives the same impression. In one week, presidents speak to a teacher's union, a chamber of commerce, a women's business council, and a group of black musicians. There is barely time for the longshoremen and the Future Farmers of America before the next week's schedule begins. The burden of the office, then, is to appear to be president of all the people by scheduling all this activity day by day.

Second, one finds the same willingness for presidents to play the role of moral and educational leader. They address specific religious groups and urge young people to pursue specific activities; in so doing they link the national government with areas of culture and religion traditionally considered outside the realm of government influence. One of the jobs of the president, judging by its annual repetition across all administrations, is to deliver a Christmas message and light a national Christmas tree.

Finally, one sees the same lack of clarity and definition seen in the major addresses as to what constitutes presidential activity. Thus, the *combination* of activities, as seen in this chapter, gives the impression that presidents may—equally and interchangeably—make appointments, conduct foreign affairs, address religious groups, and encourage particular sports or youth activities or any other areas of American culture they choose. In three days in 1969, Nixon makes a speech on campus disorders, addresses the American Cancer Society, presents a Walt Disney commemorative medal and greets the Canadian prime minister. In another few days, Carter addresses the nation on Soviet combat troops, attends a ceremony honoring family unity, speaks to a country music group, and welcomes Pope John Paul II. Perhaps the public can separate the speech on Soviet troops from the one on family unity, but the presidents themselves are not making a distinction. If it is not clear from the major addresses what presidents are supposed to do or how they have come to office, it is also not clear in the minor addresses. Presidents draw no boundaries defining or limiting their activities.

Audiences Effects

To test the effects of audience, a sample of minor addresses was selected from the first three years of each administration. The speeches show presidents addressing (1) *party groups,* members of their own political party; (2) *support groups,* those closely associated with their party or their own political background; and (3) *cross groups,* those traditionally associated with the opposite party. Thus, a labor group would be considered a support group for Democratic presidents and a cross group for Republican presidents. One speech was selected for each president for each of the three audiences.[7]

That presidents know who their friends and political opponents are is easily discernible from the speeches. Reagan explicitly identifies with the Conservative Political Action Conference he addresses (labeled *support group*). He reminisces about the meetings he attended with them before he was president, how everyone felt when Barry Goldwater was nominated, and the long road they have traveled to their present success. Eisenhower admits to the American Federation of Labor Convention (labeled *cross group*) that "there are certain things that I do of which this group as a body does not approve," and Kennedy comments wryly at a chamber of commerce meeting *(cross group)*:

> In 1960 I do not think it wholly inaccurate to say that I was the second choice of a majority of businessmen for the office of President of the United States, and when I approached the White House the cheers of members of the Chambers of Commerce around the country were not overwhelming or deafening.

Presidents, in other words, would be clearly perceiving the difference in audience as they move from one group to another.

Table 4.4 shows the relative emphasis on politics and religion in the three different kinds of groups. In speeches outside the party context, political references are infrequent, averaging one in every two pages worth of words. When politics is mentioned at all, it tends to be treated negatively; thus, without a trace of sarcasm, Eisenhower twice tells the AFL that he is glad "nothing political is expected" of him from that apolitical group. In the speech quoted previously, Kennedy does refer to 1960 (counted as a reference to the election), but he leaves it to the audience to determine how he "approached" the White House and what kind of "choice" was made. Both support groups and cross groups, then, appear to be treated similarly in the lack of political reminders, and treated the same as the nationwide audience. Only in the party group does politics appear. References average four for every page of words. The references, moreover, are not merely to Democrats and Republicans,

Table 4.4
References to Politics and Religion in Speeches to Three Different Audiences[a]

| | Number of References | | |
	Parties/Politics	God/Religion	Number of Pages
Party group	117	7	30
Support group	25	22	44
Cross group	11	11	27.5

a. *Party groups* refer to Democratic or Republican groups addressed by presidents of the same party. *Support groups* are those traditionally associated with the party of the president of closely connected with the president himself; for example, labor groups for Democratic presidents and business groups for Republicans. *Cross groups*, as the name implies, are those traditionally suporting the opposite party. All speeches are taken from the first three years of the administration. For a list of speeches, see note 7.

but include election, votes, campaign, ballots—all the reminders of a political process not discussed beyond the party doors. Audience, therefore, does appear to affect a president's willingness to mention politics, but its effect is limited to the party group. The other groups, like the nationwide audience, are not encouraged to think of presidents as political leaders, even though politics is the business that the groups and the presidents have come together to conduct.

Reagan is something of an exception. His talks to Republicans sound like his major addresses in many ways. He identifies himself with the nation, reads letters from citizens who have written to him, and keeps political references to a minimum. It is in the speeches to other conservative groups that the political talk appears. For example, in a speech to the Heritage Foundation on 3 October 1983, he talks of the past and the future presidential election. He speaks of public opinion polls and Mondale buttons, and uses words like election, victory, campaign, Democrats, and politics. In a speech to the Conservative Political Action Conference on 20 March 1981, he identifies himself as one of the group. Here the first person plural is clear and consistent. "Our memories," "our goals," "our . . . consistent philosophy" refer to conservatives. He gives some frank political advice: "I also believe that we conservatives, if we mean to continue governing, must realize that it will not always be so easy to place the blame on the past for our national difficulties." He points out that "we have to offer America and the world a larger vision," and he concludes, "Fellow citizens, fellow conservatives, our time is now. Our moment has arrived." For Reagan, the Republican party is a support group; the conservatives are his party.

Table 4.5 reports how the government is presented to the different audiences, paralleling the categories of major actors shown in table 2.3. The results are strikingly similar across groups and similar to the national addresses: Presidents present themselves as the government, with few references to Congress, department secretaries, or other administration actors. Group references increase, as would be expected, compared to the nationally broadcast speeches, as presidents acknowledge the contribution their audience has made. If one eliminates references to the particular audience being addressed, however, subnational groups appear as infrequently as they do in the national addresses, totaling less than 5 percent of the subject references for each audience. Note that the pronoun "we" is coded in the first category in the table only when it refers to the president, the nation, or the American people as a whole. Other uses of the pronoun—for example, when Reagan refers to conservatives as "we"—are included with the people the president is identifying with. Therefore, the percentages in the first row of the table may be compared directly with table 2.3. The president, the nation, and the

Table 4.5
Government Actors (Sentence Subjects) in Speeches to Three Different Audiences[a]

	Percentage of Subject References		
	Party Group	Support Group	Cross Group
We, the president, and the nation[b]	73	70	77
Congress	1	1	0
Administration, advisers	2	3	2
Subnational groups	17	19	15
Other nations, people	0	0	4
Humanity, the world	0	0	0
All other actors	7	6	2
N subject references	441	511	448

a. The groups follow the definitions in table 4.4. For a list of speeches selected, see note 7.

b. The subject "we" is coded in this category only when it refers to the nation, the American people, or the president himself. All other uses of the pronoun—as in "we" [organized labor and the administration] or "we" [Pat and I]—are coded in the category describing the actor being associated with the president: in the first example, subnational groups; and in the second example, all other actors.

American people constitute 75 percent of the major government actors in the inaugurals, 78 percent in the economic addresses, and 61 percent in the foreign policy speeches. The same actors are featured in 70 to 77 percent of the references in addresses to the party and interest groups.

The audience in these minor addresses, however, is attentive and informed about politics. Members are aware of the importance of congressional committees, access to White House aides, appointments at cabinet and subcabinet levels. They are themselves part of the activity and conflict among interest groups. So it is striking that presidents present the same picture of government to these people as they do to the broader, less politically informed electorate. "We must win" the economic battle, Ford tells the National Association of Realtors, "Republicans and Democrats alike, Nevadans and Michiganders and New Yorkers, rich and poor, black and white, young and old." In short, the audience does not appear to affect the view of government being presented. The president remains alone.

There are other reminders of the major addresses in these speeches. Nixon and Reagan quote freely from their citizen letter writers. Ford continues to take shots at his former institution, listing all the legislation that must wait "until Congress returns." Nixon talks to the American Medical Association about the nation's spiritual health. Three presidents say "the past is prologue." Always the refrain continues:

Let us begin . . .

We must go forward . . .

We'll keep moving forward . . .

We can say to the world and pledge to our children America's best days lie ahead.

Major and minor addresses differ, of course, in the degree of informality expected. Accordingly, presidents are more willing to identify themselves personally and use the first-person singular in the minor addresses than they are before a national audience. In the major addresses the plural "we" far outnumbers the singular "I," with the latter including specific references to the president's administration. In the minor addresses, by contrast, the singular outnumbers the plural: 49 percent compared to 24 percent of the references to party groups; 37 percent compared to 30 percent in the support groups; and 46 percent compared to 31 percent in the cross groups. It is not surprising that the party addresses show the highest ratio of personal references. If presidents can indulge in mentions of campaigns and elections, they can surely use personal references more freely as well. Although the plural pronoun continues to be used to link the president with the nation and the American people, the particular individual is also presented to the audience.

Johnson, Nixon, and Reagan are the most informal. They joke, mention many people by name, and tell homely stories of their family life. In a speech on inflation, Johnson recounts how he had to go out and buy a ham from "a farmer friend" for Lady Bird's Sunday night buffet. Nixon tells his groups what he has been doing that day and what he must do after he leaves them. (He will meet with the postmaster general and the prime minister of Israel and hold a national security meeting.) Few descriptions like these can be found in the major addresses. At the other extreme, Eisenhower's and Carter's speeches sound much the same as their major addresses. Carter's speech to the Democratic National Committee shortly after taking office simply lists the policies he has under way. It sounds like a shortened version of the State of the Union address he has given a few weeks before.

These differences hold for all groups addressed and not merely the party, support, and cross groups. When one looks at the longest of the minor speeches, one sees that Carter and Eisenhower are the least likely to adapt their subject matter to the audience. Carter gives broad reviews of his economic and foreign policy programs to most audiences he addresses at any length. Eisenhower discusses foreign policy at the Iowa State Fair, the Hollywood Bowl, and the American Legion, warning of the dangers of communism and outlining the nation's best response. In contrast, audience largely determines the subject matter for Kennedy and Nixon. Kennedy is politely formal with all groups, talking about programs for conservation, education, or economic policy depending on the groups addressed. Nixon is more personal and informal, discussing the problems of milk producers or senior citizens with these groups and telling football stories to his football groups. Truman and Johnson vary their approach, from broad to specific. In a tour through Oregon, Washington, and Idaho, Truman talks potatoes and atomic weapons at some stops and broad economic policy at others. In his midwestern tour of May 1950, he turns from a broad policy speech in Wisconsin to a point-by-point discussion in Ohio of farm programs. Reagan is in a class by himself when one looks at the longest addresses. Reagan gives essentially the same speech—on the Economic Mess that he is trying to correct—to all but his Central American audiences.

These findings parallel the stylistic differences seen in chapter 2, with Carter and Eisenhower found to be the most abstract and general, and Nixon direct and personal. They reinforce a point of this chapter, too, that the audience does not shape the presentation. Presidents not only pick their audiences but they decide independently of these choices what they will talk about.

It is the variety in these minor addresses that marks the major departure from the nationwide presentation. The previous chapters showed a remarkable similarity across presidents, independent of circumstances and individual styles. These minor addresses, by contrast, show considerable variety, depending on who the presidents are addressing and what they decide to say. Truman and Johnson discuss foreign policy with their support groups, accounting for most of the references to other nations in table 4.5. Ford and Eisenhower discuss party groups almost exclusively in their talks to party members, whereas Johnson talks about a number of groups, and Reagan makes no mention of parties or groups at all. Nixon gives the National Federation of Republican Women a lengthy description of what First Ladies do. (They decorate the White House, they help their husbands, they pick out the president's ties.) In contrast, Ford talks to a group of young Republicans about the Republican party generally, and Reagan reads letters from individual citizens to his Republicans, with no reference to the citizens' party affiliations. Reagan's letter writers and Nixon's family members together constitute most of the references to all other actors, as listed in the party column in table 4.5. In short, one could not say that Democratic presidents address labor groups, or all presidents address party groups, in any particular way. A considerable amount of variety is evident.

By itself, the fact may seem of minor significance. Presidents would be expected to vary their presentations depending on the time and circumstance. Nixon might feel, for example, that women who are Republican party activists would rather hear about First Ladies than presidents. Johnson may discuss foreign policy with the AFL-CIO because it is on his mind at the time. The fact is important, however, in comparison with the major addresses, where no such finding was observable. In consequence, the extreme stylization and similarity of the major addresses become all the more noticeable.

As would be expected, presidents are more informal and personal in fact-to-face groups than in nationally televised addresses. The first-person plural is outnumbered by the singular in the minor addresses, whereas it dominates the major speeches. Presidents appear less constrained to follow set patterns and speak in particular ways. Religion is emphasized less in the political groups than in the inaugurals, although in about the same proportion as in the national economic addresses. In spite of this variety, several of the main components of the presentation, as identified earlier, can be found in the minor addresses as well. Presidents present themselves as the single figure in the government. They link themselves with the nation and the American people, although less exclusively than in the major addresses. They continue to shun the mention of political activity in talks to political supporters and critics. Only to party groups do presidents admit that they engage in political activity and have come to office through election. In other words, the impression created in major addresses is not contradicted or dissipated by the minor addresses. While the style of the presentation varies, the same character and the same government are presented to the audience.

The minor speeches appear considerably more varied than the major speeches. Presidents pick their groups and, in so doing, convey a sense of individual style. Nevertheless, beyond the individual differences one finds the same emphasis on the ceremonial and religious and the same downplaying of parties and interest-group conflict. One finds, also, a lack of delineation as to what presidents are supposed to do. If they are to be all things to all people, as this chapter suggests, then the burden of the office is truly immense; but it is not necessarily a burden of government, or one that reflects a division of power in American government or society.

"We must not bother the President," Sherman Adams used to say of Eisenhower. "He is trying to keep the world from war."[8] Presidents may be doing this, in behind-the-scenes activity not reported in the *Public Papers* or in national and international speeches. But they may very likely instead be addressing the Boy Scouts, the Masons, the Future Farmers of America, presiding at a "Back to God" conference of the American

Legion, or providing the symbol of the nation and the government at other cultural and ceremonial affairs.

Are there limits that could be set on this activity, now comprising a part of every working day? In accepting or rejecting these symbolic communications, Americans can decide if this is what they want their president to be. It is not a matter of assigning these tasks to others in the White House. The vice-president and the president's wife already fulfill the lesser ceremonial duties: taking trips abroad, heading special commissions, presiding over programs for drug rehabilitation, special education, or mental illness. All of these ceremonial duties more than double the number taken in the president's name. Nor could the vice-president be given more important tasks, speaking to the American Legion or a chamber of commerce for instance, to free up the president's schedule. If the ceremonies are seen as part of the office, then assigning these tasks to others is the same as giving presidential power away. There is not room for a rival, as vice-presidents have discovered before.

Michael Novak recognizes this problem when he proposes semi-seriously that a chief of state could be elected at the beginning of each decade to preside over the ceremonies of the nation and give the decade part of its symbolic character. The president would see to the business of government while the chief of state organized scientific academies and prizes, initiated studies and commissions, and announced new national priorities and trends. The president's claim to personify the nation would thus be checked and limited by another symbolic personage. But if one can only persuade people by claiming to personify them, then presidents and other advocates of presidential power would probably not think well of the proposal.[9]

Another idea is worth raising, however. Why should the *government* or any person in government be expected to personify the cultural variety of a nation? First of all, it is probably impossible to do so. The chapter has shown that the groups who are being addressed change with the interests, hobbies, and partisanship of the president. Some groups— native Americans for example—are rarely addressed by any president. Although presidents claim to represent all of the people, they appear better at representing some than others. Moreover, the symbol alone even apart from the facts challenges a tradition in this country of cultural pluralism: a social diversity and richness that no one individual can speak for or personify. Clearly, if the head of government is considered the spokesman for the diverse institutions and social life of a nation—for its arts, medicine, religions, and family relations—the nation does not have cultural pluralism. What form of government this might be called is a matter that could be debated.

There are former baseball greats to greet the new world champions, leading artists and musicians to give artistic endowment awards. There are war heroes to talk to the American Legion and millionaires to inspire the chambers of commerce across the nation. The Boy Scouts might even prefer to meet Reggie Jackson or Darryl Strawberry than George Bush. The presidents say they can speak for all of the people, but symbols have to be both given and received.

5
The Presidents in History

The American people, if I understand them. . . .
—*William Howard Taft*

The people of the United States . . . have asked for
discipline and direction under leadership
—*Franklin Roosevelt*

The modern presidents show striking similarities in their presentation of the office. But which of these components are part of a larger historical pattern and which suggest new developments and trends? If the definition of the office has changed, at what point and through what means have these changes been arrived at? A broader historical view is needed to place these particular components in perspective and to see how the institution develops over time.

Is the modern symbolic presidency a new phenomenon, a historical hybrid, or a continuation of patterns of the past? At this point, one can find arguments, along with supporting quotations and examples, to support each point of view. Some writers say that the rise of the rhetorical presidency began in the days of Woodrow Wilson. Others date the idealized, or textbook, presidency from the time of Franklin Roosevelt and the New Deal.[1] Yet, studies can show commonalities in presidential addresses from George Washington to the present.[2] Presidents invoke a divine blessing on the nation and speak of America's special place in the world. The same continuity is seen in election campaigns and campaign biographies. According to one account, "One sees a plain, simple man of modest means, surrounded by a dutiful loving wife and adoring children; a man of practical good sense, . . . Christian piety, . . . and sturdy republican virtue." One thinks of Johnson going out shopping for the ham for Lady Bird's buffet or the Nixons celebrating a quiet anniversary watching movies of their daughter's wedding. The author concludes:[3]

> One cannot fail to be struck by the essential similarity in so many respects of all of the candidates as they appeared in campaign biographies between 1824 and 1960. That some characteristics of this symbol should be so fundamental that they would endure down through the years could of course be expected. But that so many . . . should endure was decidedly not anticipated.

Jeffrey Tulis sets forth a third possibility, combining continuity and change. In a very original argument, Tulis suggests that a process of layering has occurred by which modern presidential rhetoric has been added on to more conventional forms. He also suggests that Woodrow Wilson plays a key role in this layering process, breaking out from the conventional rhetoric in ways that the modern presidents will follow. Tulis uses selected documents to argue the point, drawing on such speakers as Washington, Lincoln, Andrew Johnson, Woodrow Wilson, and Lyndon Johnson.[4]

However, at this point it is not clear which portions of the symbolism are enduring and which represent significant changes and trends. It is also not clear at what stage and through what processes change has occurred. We do not know the age of the symbolic presidency, nor its founders and forerunners. Some systematic investigation is needed that can compare the symbolism across time.

This chapter traces the symbolism back into history. It focuses on the earlier twentieth century presidents, using comparable speeches of inaugurals and State of the Union messages.[5] One chapter clearly cannot give a full account of this period with its patterns, politics, and individual variation. Nevertheless, looking at the modern patterns only, it can identify the changes that have occurred and try to locate and explain them in time. The earlier presidents, then, can be compared with their successors for the way they present themselves to the nation.

The time span encompasses the years of Theodore Roosevelt, the first new president elected in the century, to the terms of Franklin Roosevelt. During these years the nation fights a Great War, experiences sweeping social changes, and suffers an economic collapse. There are scandals in the White House and the death of a president in office. Seven presidents take the inaugural oath. They can be compared with the eight modern presidents.

The Shifting Symbolic Patterns

Presidential Government

Much has been given us, and much will rightfully be expected from us. We have duties to others and duties to ourselves; and we can shirk neither. We have become a great nation, forced by the fact of its greatness into relations with the other nations of the earth.

While ever careful to refrain from wronging others, we must be no less insistent that we are not wronged ourselves.

If we fail, the cause of free self-government throughout the world will
rock to its foundations.

So Theodore Roosevelt delivers his inaugural address in March, 1905
in words and rhythms that will be echoed by the modern presidents.
Continuities are seen also in the way the government is presented. Like
their successors, the earlier presidents describe a presidentially dominated government. Few other actors play major roles. The frequency of
major actors cited as the subject of sentences in the inaugurals can be
seen in Table 5.1 and compared to the modern presidents. Indeed, the
earlier presidents are slightly less likely than the moderns to cite other
actors beside the president, the nation, and the American people. The
comparable figures are 22 to 25 percent. They are, however, more likely
to cite other American participants than the modern presidents are. The
ratios are 16 to 5 percent. As the modern presidents focus attention more
on other nations in the world, references to American actors decline.

Nevertheless, the table shows one sharp difference from the modern
pattern. Unlike the moderns, the earlier presidents vary greatly one from
another in the form of their presentations. Taft refers to other actors
fifty percent of the time, while Franklin Roosevelt rarely mentions them.
FDR, Hoover, and Taft refer to themselves in the first person frequently,
whereas Coolidge, Wilson, and Theodore Roosevelt do not. Although

Table 5.1
The Major Government Actors in The Early Twentieth Century[a]

			Percent of Subject References						
	TR	WT	WW	WH	CC	HH	FR	Total	Total Modern Presidents
Actor									
I, this administration	0	24	7	18	7	21	35	17	17
The nation and the American people	0	3	8	12	28	16	18	15	6
We	78	23	67	55	48	38	36	46	52
All other actors	22	50	19	15	17	25	10	22	25
American actors								(16)	(5)
Other nations, world								(5)	(16)
All other references								(1)	(4)
N subject references	18	59	27	82	90	68	40	384	421

a. Based on the first inaugural addresses of T. Roosevelt, Taft, Wilson, Harding, Coolidge, Hoover, and F. Roosevelt. The table follows the coding rules of tables 2.1 and 2.3.
American actors include Congress, administration, groups, as well as all references to the
government and the Constitution. Other references refer to the final miscellaneous category
in table 2.3.

the averages are similar to the modern presidents, there is no one typical early twentieth century address.

The former presidents are also less likely to identify with the nation through the mixing and interweaving of the world *we*. While many of the speakers use the plural form, they do so with clearer referents that do not shift within the paragraph. Most of the time the word joins the president and the American people. So Franklin Roosevelt remarks that we, as Americans, still have much to be thankful for and that we, the president and the American people, will face our common difficulties. When he speaks of the policies he favors and the proposals he will urge on Congress, he uses the singular form. Theodore Roosevelt, in many ways a very modern president, uses the plural form for both the nation and the people, although he does not join it to statements about his administration.

That these forms of presentation are not merely rhetorical patterns is seen by William Taft's inaugural address. Taft talks about the same things that the other presidents do: trade and immigration, monetary policy, the problems of race, and the need to strengthen the army and navy. He outlines the nation's foreign policy and the challenges to the administration in the days ahead. Yet, while the content is the same, the form is sharply different, as seen by the sentence subjects. The government, as Taft presents it, has a Congress (four references) as well as departments and commissions (six references). There have been presidents before Taft (three references to presidents in general) and even a predecessor whom he mentions twice. While references to himself and the nation comprise fifty percent of the subjects, there is more to the government, Taft makes clear, than a president. The Constitution itself is the subject of four sentences. The word *Constitution* is used once more as subject, in a 1933 address. It then virtually disappears from the inaugural speeches until Gerald Ford finds occasion to use it in 1974.

Taft made clear by his acts in office and later writings that he opposed the kind of aggrandized office favored by his predecessor, Theodore Roosevelt. Known as a strict constructionist of the Constitution, Taft argued that there was no undefined residuum of power that presidents could exercise when it seemed to them to be in the public interest. The notion that presidents should "play the part of a Universal Providence and set all things right" he saw as an unsafe doctrine that could threaten individual rights. The president, he observed, cannot make clouds to rain and cannot make corn to grow; he cannot make business good.[6] The contrasting views of the office held by Taft and Theodore Roosevelt are reflected in the structure of their inaugurals as shown in the Table. The government, as Roosevelt portrays it, is centered in a president who speaks so completely for the nation and the American people that they do not need to be mentioned separately. Taft's picture of government is more complex and dispersed among many different actors. While the president is of central importance, with fully one half of the subject references, there is a Constitution, a Congress, and executive departments also at work.

Another exceptional view of the presidency is seen in Franklin Roosevelt's first inaugural. This view, like Taft's, will not become the dominant modern form. FDR cites very few other actors as sentence subject—fewer in fact than any other twentieth century president. At the same time, however, he uses a very high proportion of first person singular references, more than all of the other twentieth century presidents except Ford. (Ford's reasons for using this form are explained in Chapter 2.) The structure suggests a personalized leadership held in Roosevelt's own hands. The ideas expressed in the inaugural support this view.

Roosevelt sets forth his view of his role in the opening lines of the address:

> In every dark hour of our national life a leadership of frankness and vigor has met with that understanding and support of the people themselves which is essential to victory. I am convinced that you will again give that support to leadership in these critical days.

Roosevelt's role is to lead the nation out of the dark days of the depression. The word *leadership* is used five times in this short speech. That this is to be no ordinary leadership is seen by the remark that the money changers have been driven from the temple. For their part, the American people's role is to accept discipline and give Roosevelt support. The words *discipline* and *duty* are used eight times. The same view is repeated in conclusion. The people have asked for discipline and direction under Roosevelt's leadership. They have made him the instrument of their wishes. He therefore accepts the gift. Just as George Washington told his audience what he wished to be famous for, Franklin Roosevelt tells people he will lead them out of the depression years. He will be famous for vigorous action and leadership.

This is actually quite an exceptional document in American history. Although Roosevelt refers once to a mandate from the people, there is no other hint throughout the address that the country has a democratic form of government. His references to the Constitution prepare for the statement that he may need to take extra-constitutional actions to meet the emergency. He reminds people of the "clean satisfaction that comes from the stern performance of duty by old and young alike" and pictures the American people moving "as a trained and loyal army willing to sacrifice for the good of a common discipline." The people will submit their lives and property to this leadership because it aims at a larger good. The speech seems closer to those of other leaders who are rising to power in the 1930s than to those of American presidents.

The Roosevelt and Taft illustrations need not represent the only alternatives to the modern presidency. It is true that they pose extremes of power: in one case, a power carefully limited by a written constitution; in the other, power given by the people to an individual leader, who accepts it without condition. Still, there should be many ways to present the office and the relationships linking the people, the nation, and the government. At the same time, the illustrations show a variety of pictures of government available through the early years of the century, a variety that contrasts sharply with the modern addresses. The presidents following FDR have many models to pick and choose from. The illustrations also show how the structure of action as analyzed here can reveal clues about the various presidencies that accord with other evidence.

The modern speakers show little difference between the inaugurals and State of the Union addresses, in each case presenting a government in which presidents stand alone. In contrast, the earlier presidents show a distinct pattern in their State of the Union messages. They are *policy* speeches primarily, setting forth for the Congress both agenda priorities and details of programs. These addresses, so different from the inaugurals, require a separate investigation. They can be compared with the modern messages, for the third year of the first elected term.

The results for the State of the Union messages are summarized in Table 5.2. Overall, the presidents portray a government divided among many actors. While the president is centrally important, with fully one half of the subject references, other people are shown at work in the government, too. This follows the Taft pattern as seen in the inaugural speeches. Whereas the modern presidents refer to other actors about one fourth of the time, the earlier presidents feature them twice as often. The difference holds when the earlier State of the Union addresses are compared with the modern foreign and economic policy speeches.

The most dramatic difference is seen for the category of government and administration actors. The former presidents speak frequently of what the national government should do, making clear that this government is separate from themselves. Theodore Roosevelt talks of how the national government can correct child labor practices and protect resources. Harding discusses how the government should manage the coal industry. Even Hoover explains how the government is fighting unemployment by programs of public-building, harbor, highway, aviation, and ship construction. Appropriations for these projects have more than tripled in three years. In each of these cases presidents show the

Table 5.2
Major Government Actors in State of the Union Messages[a]

	Percent Subject References									
	Earlier Presidents							Modern Presidents		
	TR	WT	WW	CC	HH	FDR	Total Earlier Presidents	State of the Union	Eco- nomic Policy	For- eign Policy
We, the President and the Nation	37	48	71	47	58	78	50	76	78	65
Congress	2	3	3	8	1	0	4	2	7	1
Government, Administration	32	28	12	24	19	3	24	3	4	3
Subnational Groups	19	9	6	11	13	12	13	7	8	3
Other Nations	3	9	8	3	2	3	5	9	0	19
World, Humanity	3	1	0	3	1	0	2	1	0	1
All other Actors	3	2	0	4	5	3	3	2	3	9
N Subject References	264	207	100	148	89	60	868	1441	1306	1204

a. To parallel the modern presidents, State of the Union messages are taken from the third year of the first elected term. Harding, who died before this address could be given, is excluded.

government at work on a policy problem—a government that is much larger than themselves. These speakers also talk about particular government agencies. Cabinet departments, with the secretaries mentioned by name, carry out policies and make recommendations. Tariff boards, monetary commissions, a Panama Canal Zone commission, and the Biological Survey all make reports. Theodore Roosevelt is not building the Panama Canal by himself—at least one dozen other individuals and agencies are mentioned in his report. Coolidge outlines the action taken to meet a farm crisis, with the departments of Agriculture and Labor, the Farm Loan Board, and the Federal Reserve all taking part.

Interest groups are also very active, appearing with twice the frequency of the modern years. Theodore Roosevelt talks about ranchers, farmers, trusts, employers, and those who destroy forests, among others. Taft discusses railroads, utilities, and the need for government corporations. Coolidge covers most of the major interests, including veteran and negro groups. Wilson warns of the danger of dissident groups, primarily immigrants, who may not be loyal to the country. Franklin Roosevelt explains what must be done for those who are unemployed. These groups, it is clear, do not add up to equal the American people: they have specific interests in policies which the presidents either favor or oppose.

The number of references declines through the years as the speeches themselves become shorter.[7] Nevertheless, the differences between the early and modern periods still hold when these declining numbers are controlled for. Taking an average of each president's percentage—that is, counting each president once—yields a figure of 57 percent for the presidential references (the first row in Table 5.2), 20 percent for the category of government and administration (the third row), and 12 percent for the subnational groups. These figures are still far from the modern results.

The patterns identified hold for four of the six presidents shown in the Table as well as for Harding in his final State of the Union address.[8] Wilson and Franklin Roosevelt, however, are like the modern speakers in their portrayal of a dominant presidential government. Wilson makes few references to groups, and Franklin Roosevelt barely mentions the government or administration. Wilson's speech, it should be understood, is not merely the result of a president preparing the nation for war. Wilson gives the same short, general address in both his first and second annual messages. The shifting pictures of government seen in the inaugurals are seen even more clearly in these addresses.

Theodore Roosevelt's message, in fact, is different enough from his contemporaries, to suggest a distinct type of its own. Roosevelt speaks about the president and the nation so rarely—37 percent of the time— because he is talking about specific policies of government. The proposals he calls for in this 1907 address will provide the legislative agenda for the next third of the century. He asks for workers' compensation and laws regulating the employment of women and children. A bureau of mines should be created, national forests set aside, and new waterways constructed. Laws are needed to govern the northwest territory and Alaska. The medical corps of the army needs to be professionalized. National campaign finance is called for and a national gallery of art. All this is supplied in detail far beyond that which Jimmy Carter would later be criticized for. Roosevelt explains just how the army medical ranks should be reassigned, with the expertise needed for each rank. He points out how he has arrived at the judgement that the correct width for the locks in the Gatun dam should be 120 feet.

Here is the vision and policy leadership often called for by writers on the presidency, but it is presented without the symbols usually thought to signify that leadership. It is not the president, but the policies, that are the dominant feature of the address. Roosevelt does not need to say we shall go forward, because his agenda is moving the nation forward into the new age.

Politics and Morality

Sharp changes across the century occur as presidents present themselves as political and moral leaders. The political words—party, election, mandate, votes—heard so rarely in the modern inaugurals are much more frequent in the earlier addresses. Whereas the modern presidents average barely one reference for every two pages of an inaugural address, the earlier presidents average more than three references. Shifting patterns are also apparent. Theodore Roosevelt, Harding, and Franklin Roosevelt make very few political references, while Wilson and Coolidge give a great many. Taft and Hoover make a moderate number, although still twice as many as the modern presidents. The use of political words appears independent of time and the party of the president in office.

A tradition is followed by most of the former presidents that contrasts sharply with the modern pattern. For these speakers, the inauguration is an occasion to explain their electoral mandate. They need not mention the word *mandate,* but they must explain what it is. As Taft sets forth the tradition, it is "the office of the address" to outline the policies of the new administration and to relate them to the platform of the party elected to the White House. Coolidge says that his administration has come into power with a clear mandate from the people. He goes on to detail what these policies are. Hoover says it is a "tradition throughout our history" for the newly elected president to explain his policies, and that governments should carry out the platforms of the party entrusted to power. He then explains the platforms—on the eighteenth amendment, courts, education, public health and foreign policy. Wilson begins his first inaugural not with a prayer or request for divine blessing, but with the words,

> There has been a change of government. It began two years ago, when the House of Representatives became Democratic by a decisive majority. It has now been completed. The Senate about to assemble will also be Democratic. The offices of President and Vice-President have been put into the hands of Democrats. What does this change mean? . . . That is the question I am going to try to answer, in order, if I may, to interpret the occasion.

Wilson goes on to review the things that must be changed and those that must be strengthened. The nation is using the Democratic Party to interpret a change in its plans and point of view.

Even Franklin Roosevelt interprets what the election means for his personal leadership of the nation, although he does not mention that an election occurred. Harding speaks of his policies in general terms. Theodore Roosevelt marks the only exception to the practice, in his first inaugural speaking only of the greatness of the nation, its past blessings, and great responsibilities. This address could be copied directly for use by the modern presidents.

The president is a party leader according to most of the earlier speakers. The election and inauguration are directly linked for all of the presidents but one. Inaugurals therefore should state the policies that the presidents were elected for. Somehow, by Truman's 1949 inaugural the tradition has been lost and the link between election and inauguration is broken.

While politics has declined, religion has risen sharply. The comparable figures are shown in Table 5.3. The modern presidents are three times more likely than there predecessors to use religious words and phrases. Indeed all of the modern presidents except Truman outrank all of the earlier presidents in the religious emphasis given the inaugurals. On this dimension Truman fits more with his predecessors than with the presidents since Eisenhower. The point will be returned to later in the chapter. The rankings follow according to average references per page:

Modern Presidents		Former Presidents
Eisenhower	11	
Nixon	10	
Ford	9	
Johnson	8	
Carter	8	
Kennedy	7	
Reagan	6	
	5	Franklin Roosevelt
	3	Harding
	3	Theodore Roosevelt
Truman	2	Wilson
	2	Coolidge
	2	Hoover
	.4	Taft

When moral and religious references are combined, the modern presidents still outdo the earlier speakers by a ratio of two to one. Wilson and Theodore Roosevelt are high on combined references, tying with Nixon and Ford, but still unable to match the Eisenhower record. For comparative purposes it is interesting to see that George Washington also ties Nixon and Ford in his first inaugural, although Abraham Lincoln ranks

Table 5.3
Religion, Morality, and Politics Compared for the Earlier and Modern Presidents[a]

| | | | Number of References | | | | |
| | | Politics | | Religion | | Religion and Morality Combined | |
	Pages	N	Per Page	N	Per Page	N	Per Page
T. Roosevelt	2.0	0	0	6	3.0	23	11.5
Taft	10.0	13	1.3	4	0.4	10	1.0
Wilson	3.0	13	4.3	7	2.3	37	12.0
Harding	6.5	0	0	21	3.2	39	6.0
Coolidge	8.0	27	3.4	14	1.8	24	3.0
Hoover	8.0	13	1.6	13	1.6	35	4.4
F. Roosevelt	3.5	1	0.3	16	4.6	32	9.1
Earlier Presidents	Average per Two Pages	3		4		10	
Modern Presidents	Average per Two Pages	1		14		20	

a. Inaugural addresses only. The table follows the measurement and coding rules in table 3.3.

with Taft in the lowest position. Lincoln's second inaugural includes many more religious references than his first.

The former presidents are quite similar to each other in religious references, as the Table makes clear. Most of the speakers invoke the aid of God in discharging their duties, although some spend longer on this invocation than others. Taft's reference consists of a single sentence. Many of the presidents also describe the nation as divinely blessed, especially in its origins. To this basic tradition, which accounts for much of the similarity among the speakers, presidents add a few unique devices. Theodore Roosevelt speaks about duty and responsibility, using these words seven times in a two-page address. Wilson uses a variety of moral and religious words to describe the evils that have come to government and their spiritual costs. The new administration must cleanse and purify the nation, correcting the evil without impairing the good. Harding's religious words describe political ideas: the temple of democracy, a benediction of understanding, the divine inspiration of the founding fathers. Franklin Roosevelt uses biblical metaphors: the money changers and a plague of locusts. None of these devices are copied in other addresses. Nor do any of these speakers pray on the platform or read scriptural verses.

The basic tradition will be greatly expanded on by the modern speakers. Modern presidents state the nation's mission in the world, describing this mission in religious terms. The earlier presidents show no consistency in this practice. Wilson, it is interesting to see, discusses no foreign policy in his first inaugural, concentrating instead on domestic issues. Indeed, he comments to a friend a few weeks before taking office, "It would be an irony of fate if my administration had to deal with foreign problems, for all my preparation has been in domestic matters."[9] FDR also stays with his urgent domestic agenda, looking back at this with astonishment in his 1936 annual message, devoted almost entirely to foreign affairs. Hoover and Taft make no mention of a mission in their inaugurals, merely repeating the nation's peaceful intent. The nation seeks peace although it must be prepared for war. Theodore Roosevelt says only that the nation is forced by the fact of its greatness into relations with other nations. It is left to Coolidge and Harding to provide the eloquence on the subject.

For Harding, the nation is a temple of democracy that can provide inspiration and example to other nations: indeed, it is divinely instituted to provide this example. The framers did not so much engineer a government as receive inspiration about what the government should be. Twice in the speech Harding refers to the world as riveting its gaze on America and "the great truths on which the founders wrought." International organizations are not helpful, Harding believes, since peace can come only when other nations establish a freedom like our own. For Coolidge "America seeks no earthly empire built on blood and force. . . . The legions which she sends forth are armed, not with the sword, but with the cross." He does not make clear how actively these legions are at work bringing other nations to the light. The words could support a passive foreign policy or one of great missionary zeal. Still, he points out that the only supranational government the country supports has a divine and not a human origin. He also reminds his audience that after World War I, "we withdrew to our shores unrecompensed save in the consciousness of duty done." This is a direct restatement, presumably unconscious, of the George Washington legend, seen in the introductory chapter.

Even if one looks further in the speeches of Wilson and Theodore Roosevelt, stronger statements of a mission rarely appear. Roosevelt is an active foreign policy participant and the first American to win a Nobel peace prize. Wilson is cheered through Europe in 1918 as the American president who seeks to bring peace to the world. Nevertheless, the actions of these presidents speak louder than their words. Roosevelt's speeches concentrate on pragmatic foreign policy proposals. Wilson, who has moved slowly from supporting neutrality to calling for a declaration of war, also moves cautiously in his speeches. He observes in a Memorial Day address in 1917 that American "was born to serve mankind," but does not specify what kind of service this should be. The famous lines used in his message asking for a declaration of war, that "the world must be made safe for democracy," are carefully cast in the passive voice while the principles of democracy at stake are not explained. Wilson has been talking about making the world safe from German submarines. America's role emerges somewhat more clearly by 1919. On a speaking tour of western states to mobilize support for the League of Nations, he does say, "We have come to redeem the world by giving it liberty and justice." The words have clear religious meaning. In his final State of the Union address, he explains how the United States must lead to make the spiritual principles of democracy prevail. By this time, of course, Wilson's health is shattered and the issue of joining the League is dead.

Symbolic statements can provide a substitute for something that does not otherwise exist. In this case the more grandiose the statement of the nation's mission by the presidents before World War II, the narrower is the actual role. Both Coolidge and Harding defend an isolationist foreign policy of no entangling alliances and no world government. Yet, Wilson's words have described how European crowds have cheered an American president. That picture is vivid enough to remain with Harding and Coolidge and to stay in the imagination of modern presidents. If the president is a synonym for the nation as the modern speakers assert, then America has taken her place as a world leader at the end of World War I amid European cheers.

The earlier presidents made foreign policy in a world where the sides and the stakes were unclear. It is not surprising, then, that the national mission was often stated in carefully guarded terms. With the onset of Word War II, the situation was changed. In Franklin Roosevelt's 1942 State of the Union message, the war is described as a conflict between good and evil. Americans are fighting with other nations to be true to a divine heritage, inspired by a faith which goes back to the first chapter of *Genesis*. They are fighting "to cleanse the world of ancient evils, ancient ills." Still, the statement of a mission is no more a dominant motif in the speeches of Roosevelt than it is for the other early presidents. It will become dominant in the inaugurals of the first three modern presidents, when, with a new enemy, freedom is still pitted against slavery and light against dark.

Like foreign policy, domestic policy is only rarely treated in moral and religious terms. One exception is Wilson's first inaugural, already described, in which the entire domestic agenda is cast as a necessary cleansing and purification of evil. A second exception, and a forerunner of later economic speeches, is provided by Franklin Roosevelt in his first inaugural address. Part of the cause of the economic collapse, Roosevelt suggests, is a failure of morality. "Small wonder that confidence languishes," he says, "for it thrives only on honesty, on honor, on the sacredness of obligations . . . on unselfish performance." Adjectives are piled on top of each other: callous, unscrupulous, stubborn, selfish. The spiritual failure extends beyond bankers and business people to the public as a whole, who has followed false leaders and held to false values. Americans have prized money and profit rather than looking to unselfish aims. The Depression was worth it, Roosevelt observes, to teach that "our true destiny is not to be ministered unto but to minister to ourselves and to our fellow men." No mention is made of world-wide economic trends. Roosevelt goes on to explain that the restoration will take more than a change in ethics, but the point has been made. Later he reassures his audience that the American people have not failed, leaving the lingering doubt that they have failed in some moral way. Certainly, an audience told to look to its sins will be more receptive to Roosevelt's call for discipline and sacrifice. The economic speeches of the modern presidents—facing federal deficits and runaway inflation—will continue this tradition.

The State of the Union addresses do not discuss politics or religion. Since the link between elections and policy has been made in the inaugural, the State of the Union messages can concentrate on what the policies are. Contrary to conventional wisdom, the practice of proposing a legislative agenda to Congress does not begin with the modern presidents. Theodore Roosevelt calls for anti-trust legislation, staking out a careful distinction between trusts and ordinary corporations. Among other proposals, he calls for tough new labor legislation, major appropriations for waterway projects, and a strengthening of the army and navy. Taft follows with the length and detail of his predecessor's address. He proposes changes in the anti-trust laws that would create government corporations and a federal corporation commission. He explains his tariff bill and reviews American foreign policy, country by country around the globe, calling for a merchant marine and a reorganization of the foreign service corps. A monetary reform bill will go to Congress with a recommendation for a National Reserve Association. Tolls should be taken on the Panama Canal, and there should be rural service for parcel post. Wilson's address in 1915 concentrates on foreign affairs and calls for a major defense buildup. Yet, he reminds the Congress of his domestic agenda from the previous session, so vital to the nation at this time of crisis. At minimum, the illustrations show that Congress could expect presidents to propose a legislative agenda long before Harry Truman came to office.

In both inaugural and State of the Union speeches the former presidents make clear that their primary role is one of policy maker. They are not the religious and cultural leaders of the nation, but the chief policy makers, charged by the election with the task of explaining these policies and putting them into effect.

The comparisons of the chapter show sharp changes over time in the presentation of the office. The electoral connection, so central to previous inaugurals, virtually disappears in the modern period. At the same time, the emphasis on morality and religion becomes much stronger. All of the modern presidents except Truman outrank all of the former presidents in their role as religious leader. In contrast to the consistency of the modern years, the earlier speakers show a variety of patterns by which they present themselves and the government. These differences are found in both inaugural and State of the Union messages. Franklin Roosevelt's pattern of individual leadership, Theodore Roosevelt's of vision and policy leadership, Taft's more complex view of a constitutional government—each provide models that are sharply different from each other and from the modern presidency. To understand the office and the potential for change over time, we need to try to explain why these changes have occurred.

The Roosevelt Interlude

A few partial explanations suggest themselves at the outset. First, the office of the president is growing substantially in the Truman and Eisenhower years,[10] and among the duties delegated to the growing number of staff people is the writing of speeches. While the earlier presidents had advisers available to write portions of speeches, or even entire addresses,[11] by the Eisenhower and Kennedy administrations the task was clearly one to be assigned to others.[12] The speeches themselves became institutionalized, as writers copied from the past public record and followed their expectations of what a president should say. This helps explain the consistency of the modern pattern in contrast to the past. Since the writers were subject to the same socialization, the expectations and the results were the same. The modern speakers, of course, could add anything they wished to the basic formulas, as earlier chapters showed. Eisenhower composed his own prayer.[13] Carter's speeches showed a negativism and Reagan's a casualness that were not found in the other addresses. Despite this surface variety, the basic formulas remained.

A second explanation points to the changing audience of these speeches. Presidential addresses were broadcast on radio since 1923, when Calvin Coolidge was in office,[14] although radio did not reach a mass audience until the end of the decade. Franklin Roosevelt clearly had a radio audience for his presidency while Truman faced both radio and television. Presidents would no longer speak only to Congress or to the small audience collected at the inaugural, they would address "the American people," who would be listening and watching across the nation. This change in audience can help explain the reluctance to discuss electoral politics or the conflict among interest groups. Since the speakers could address the people directly, they would wish to claim they were president of all the people as well. One can speculate, too, that the religious emphasis was a natural consequence of this shift in audience. Speechmaking is not a popular art form among Americans, nor are speeches by members of Congress held to the same standards of quality and style as those in some other democracies. Indeed, the only speeches many Americans may have been familiar with were those given from a religious pulpit. Hence the sermon may have become a kind of unconscious model for the presidents.

As attractive as this explanation may seem, it remains a partial one. Audiences did not change the basic presentation, the preceding chapter showed, even when the presidents spoke directly to interest groups. The two explanations together do somewhat better. With the modern presidents' schedule, speeches need to be mass produced. Formulas that are found to be effective can be copied from one address to another, independent of context, audience, or administration. This can account for *why* presentations have taken a particular form, but it does not explain *how* they came to do so—how this development was instituted across time.

Many people believe that the presidency is shaped by the great individuals of history. Lincoln, Wilson, Franklin Roosevelt—all left an office different from the one they inherited. Succeeding presidents had only to follow them. If this is the case, we would expect there to be a founder of the modern symbolic presidency, one individual to point to and say the pattern starts here. So far in the chapter, no obvious founder is apparent. Franklin Roosevelt is the first, since Wilson, to speak of the government as predominantly presidential. Truman is the first to break the connection between the inaugural and the election. Eisenhower gives religion a new central place in the White House. It is woven into his speeches and instituted in silent prayers to be held at the beginning of cabinet meetings. Yet, all three accord with tradition in other ways—they are as much followers as innovators. In contrast to Eisenhower who formally joined a church only when he became president,[15] Truman appears from his private papers to be very religious. He speaks of using principles of the Bible, naming *Exodus* XX and *Matthew* V, VI, and VII, to save the morals of the world from the Communist menace. He makes frequent mention of his Baptist and masonic traditions. Often he asks for divine guidance, saying once in characteristic fashion, "What the hell am I to do? I'll know when the time comes because I am sure God Almighty will guide me."[16] The absence of religion from the public statements, therefore, does not stem from a lack of feeling on the subject: Truman apparently believes that religion is not an appropriate subject for a presidential address.

Yet, Franklin Roosevelt's speeches deserve a closer look, not only because he is the likely candidate for founder, but because he was in office so long. The Roosevelt interlude lasts from 1933 to 1945, half again as long as any two-term president spends in office. During that time the country changed from a nation in the first years of the Depression to one emerging from victory in World War II. If in 1949, the newly elected Truman had looked for a model other than Roosevelt, he would need to go back twenty years.

Roosevelt exhibits a variety in his speeches in line with his predecessors. No one model or set of devices predominates. While some State of the Union messages make general statements only, others—the fourth annual message for example—supply a full policy agenda. Still others, like the sixth and seventh messages, follow Wilson in concentrating on foreign affairs and preparing the nation for war. During the course of these years he finds occasion to show how interest groups add together to become American people: "All of us in this Government represent the fixed-income group just as much as we represent business owners, workers, and farmers." This device, however, is not frequently repeated. He also finds occasion to state the nation's mission. As previously described, the nation is engaged in an apocalyptic conflict between good and evil: "We are fighting to cleanse the world of ancient evils, ancient ills." But these words, spoken in 1942, are descriptive and not merely rhetorical. They describe how Roosevelt and many other people throughout the world saw the stakes involved in World War II.

The inaugurals also change with the circumstances of the time. The first inaugural, previously discussed, is a model of individual leadership, with its use of the singular first person pronoun and the word *leadership* repeated throughout. The second inaugural carries this leadership forward. He no longer needs to drive the money changers from the temple, for, in a shift of religious imagery, he has led his people far but not yet to the promised land. Roosevelt then describes his vision of the road ahead, beginning with the famous lines, "I see a great nation, upon a great continent. . . ." In the vision that Roosevelt paints, he evokes the greatness of the nation, but also shows the millions who are ill-housed, ill-nourished, and ill-clad. At the same time, the speech reminds his audience of how far the nation has come in four years. It speaks about the past as much as the future. The word *leadership* is used only once. The plural pronoun, now used more frequently than the singular, describes what the nation with Roosevelt as president has been able to accomplish:

> We did those first things first.
> We have made the exercise of all power more democratic. . . .
> We must carry on.

While the pronoun is a favorite among newly elected modern presidents, Roosevelt uses it merely to describe a joint undertaking which has occurred.

Circumstances have changed greatly by the third inaugural, in 1941. The New Deal has reached a point of consolidation, and growing resistance in Congress. The nation is on the verge of war. Two weeks earlier, in his State of the Union message, Roosevelt has explained the unprecedented threat to American security and the need for defense. This speech, therefore, addresses no policy agenda but merely offers general inspirational words. Leadership is not mentioned, but *spirit* is used seven times. There is no use of the singular pronoun. The focus is almost entirely on the past with three references to George Washington, two to Lincoln, along with the Declaration of Independence, the Mayflower Compact, and the Magna Carta. Here, of course, is the model for the modern presidents, with words and phrases that will be reshuffled many times in the years ahead. The fourth inaugural, delivered from the porch of the White House by a dying president, is short and personal. It expresses faith in the future of the country under God.

Technically, Roosevelt does leave the office changed in the sense that the third inaugural, with its broad inspirational statements, comes after the first. His first address connects the inaugural to the election; the later addresses do not. Yet, many of his models are not followed, and the variety he offers will not be heard again. From the variety of speeches, produced by this master of rhetorical form, the modern presidents select what they wish, paraphrasing some things and discarding others. Thus it is not Roosevelt so much who is the founder of the modern symbolism as those who do the selecting. Truman and Eisenhower, replacing the Nazi menace with a Communist one, can find the inaugural model they need in Roosevelt's ninth annual message. Each side of the conflict is described in turn along with its intentions and beliefs. In the stark contrasts of 1942, one side is good and one is evil. Elsewhere, road metaphors are available (in the second inaugural) for Republican presidents to use as they explain why the nation must not continue to follow the New Deal. Roosevelt has even said, "We go forward." This occurs, as might be expected, in the address that looks to the inspiration of the past.

Roosevelt is copied in speeches and other things not only because of the quality of his example or reputation as a great president, but because of the duration of his term: he imposes such a large span of time between the modern presidents and the previous office holders. The earlier speeches still provide models. Lincoln's are copied; Theodore Roosevelt's inaugural is very modern; even Harding has his echoes across the years. However, the most recent examples and the most relevant ones are Roosevelt's. As recent examples and followed, earlier traditions can be lost. In his first inaugural, Roosevelt recognizes the tradition of explaining the mandate from his election. He does not do so in later inaugurals, assuming with some justification that the mandate still stands. The tradition, therefore, is not so much declined by the modern presidents as it is buried with the passage of time.

Together, these three explanations help explain the differences between the modern and earlier periods. With the delegation of speechwriting to others, a process of institutionalization and homogenization takes place. The speeches become more like each other. The Roosevelt interlude marks a sharp break with the past and provides its own excellent models for the speechwriters to follow. The writers look to Roosevelt's speeches and selected earlier examples to make the presidents sound "presidential" to a mass public audience. But why are some speeches followed and not others? How is an understanding of "presidential" arrived at? This book has argued that expectations about the office shape how it is presented; these presentations in turn affect future expectations. Roosevelt helps to shape these expectations, but it is the modern presidents who are defining the office by the examples they select.

By this explanation the symbolic presidency, *seen as a consistent way of presenting the office,* is new, best dated from the Truman-Eisenhower years. Franklin Roosevelt is not consistent in this presentation: He varies greatly across the years of his administration, following earlier styles in some things while experimenting with his own unique style in others. Roosevelt is a forerunner, as are Wilson and Theodore Roosevelt. According to the tables shown in the chapter, Wilson is most like the modern presidents in his use of moral and religious words and his emphasis on a dominant presidential government. He is unlike them, however, in speaking of parties and elections, and is overshadowed in the inaugurals by Theodore Roosevelt in identifying the president with the nation and the American people. The real founders are the modern speechwriters who, combing the past record for inspiration, select what sounds presidential to them.

This does not deny that there are important continuities with the past. Indeed, work in this book and elsewhere could be expanded to trace more completely the origin and course of the modern symbols. Yet, earlier chapters have shown sharp breaks with the past: in the matter of election mandates, constitutional principles, or reminders that there is a Constitution. Speeches stating these principles—Ford's pardon of Nixon, Kennedy's nationalizing of state troops—are the exceptions. Much more commonly, as in the Eisenhower speech quoted earlier, these become "the principles of faith by which we live," with faith carrying many nonconstitutional meanings. Ronald Reagan was the president most willing to mention history in his addresses. Those who heard his first inaugural would know that there were presidents before Reagan, including Washington, Lincoln, and Franklin Roosevelt. They would know that American history included many wars, a building economic crisis, and something called a Declaration of Independence; but they would not learn anything about a Constitution or its principles. The modern speeches seem less a hybrid of earlier and recent forms, as Tulis has argued, than a selection, often deliberate, of which forms will be followed.

The modern symbolism is not locked in place by the time of the Truman presidency. Truman appears to be the first to read letters from individual citizens. Eisenhower makes religion a dominant part of the inaugural address. If one counts all the inaugural addresses, Franklin Roosevelt stands between the earlier and later presidents in religious emphasis, outranking only Truman among the modern speakers. Eisenhower, then, is carrying on a tradition at the same time he is bringing it to a new level. Other trends, not yet identified, could also be taking place. Nevertheless, the homogenization of speeches suggests that the changes should be fewer in the contemporary period. Even if some future president did bring a new vision to the office, there would be no twelve-year interlude to bury the traditions of the past.

To explain an event is not to justify it. The modern symbolic presidency has been shaped by the Roosevelt interlude, a change in audience, and the institutionalization of speechwriting. It has also been shaped by public expectations of what the office should be. The dynamic point remains the expectations. Change can occur if the symbolism is questioned by the public to which the presidents and the speechwriters are so closely attuned.

Other Comparisons

The variety shown for the presidents across the century has wider implications. The results of the earlier chapters are not a structural or rhetorical artifact: There are differences in presentation which tell more about the institution and how it changes across time. A set of broader questions, then, are raised by the results of this chapter. Since presidents are not alone in making symbolic presentations, additional comparisons are indicated.

How do presidents differ from other American leaders? Which components can be attributed to a broader public philosophy and which appear uniquely presidential—office related—traits? One could hypothesize that presidents alone identify with the nation, an identification that ends when they leave the White House. All political leaders in American society may shun the political, invoke morality, and enlist in their cause God and the great figures of the nation's history. But one might also expect that these leaders would be more willing than the modern presidents to mention other governmental actors, discuss the recent past, and acknowledge the existence of controversy. In other words, the picture of American politics presented by these other leaders may be more detailed and factually based than the picture presented by the presidents.

Do presidents differ from other elected officials, such as governors and members of Congress, in speaking for their constituencies? If presidents identify with the nation and its people, do governors similarly speak for the state? More plausibly, given the notion that the president is somehow unique and exceptional, one might suspect that only presidents engage in this identification. Representatives, according to Richard Fenno, present themselves as part of the district, one of the people in the district. They belong to it and seek to help it in the harsh world of Washington politics. But nothing in Fenno's study suggests that they speak for it or presume to cast themselves as equivalent with it.[17] Would governors, in contrast to presidents, be willing to mention other state government actors, discuss past administrations, and acknowledge controversy? Are presidents, in short, like other American elected officials in their presentation of themselves and the political universe, or is their dramatization the exception?

To what extent are presidents similar to other heads of state? The declaration "L'État—c'est moi" was not coined by a modern American president, and ex-leaders may find themselves expunged from history in both democratic and non-democratic regimes. Governments throughout history have used religion to provide political legitimacy. Thus,

> Religious myths serve as referents for political rhetoric and ritual in order to provide a symbolic base for legitimation. In other words, clothing the state in religious garments and investing government with the rich robes of godliness yields popular acceptance.[18]

Presidents, then, may be merely engaging in traditional executive devices to gain support for their administration. But if indeed they are like other heads of state and unlike other American political officials, two ironies will follow. First, the very uniqueness of this democratic head of state would be undercut: He would, in effect, be no different from any other. Second, any pride in a form of government characterized by pluralism and a separation of powers would be challenged if legitimacy could be achieved only at the price of seeming to be ruled, not by the many, but by one.

Finally, presidents need to be compared with nonpolitical leaders.

Popular religious figures address a wide public audience, often on nationally broadcast television. They pray, make theological statements, and cast political questions in religious and moral terms. Indeed, as the audiences of the two kinds of leaders have become more similar—a mass public audience reached through television—the content and form of the speeches may be mirroring each other. The presidents grow more religious as the television evangelists become political. In preparing his inaugural address, John Kennedy solicited a list of biblical quotations from Billy Graham.[19] Richard Nixon was an even greater admirer of Graham, attending several functions in his honor within a twelve-month period in the White House. Presumably the television evangelists, vying for their own popularity, watch for the most effective presidential symbols. Can the president's religious leadership be distinguished from other religious activity, and are there differences of degree or of kind? Are presidents more similar to religious leaders than to other elected public officials?

The comparisons of this chapter can help place the results in perspective. All presidents make some reference to religion, although the extent of the emphasis varies greatly. It is therefore not enough to say that many political speakers use religion to gain legitimacy. Do they make a few obligatory references, like Taft, or a great many, like Eisenhower and Nixon, so that religion appears a central part of the government? It is expected that most national executives addressing an audience would be high on self references, whether they present themselves personally or as one with the nation and its people. But how frequent are these self references—are they like Taft's or a modern presidential inaugural? Do other executives provide a personal leadership or do they identify with the nation? Do they provide a policy agenda for the future or inspiration from the past?

These questions can be extended and formalized to a series of hypotheses about the modern presidential office. If the office is unlike other American political offices, one would expect (1) sharp differences between presidents and other political speakers in the number of actors cited, the extent of controversy referred to, and the kind of identification made; and (2) considerable similarity among the other speakers on these dimensions. If the office is like other national executive offices, independent of the form of government, one would expect (3) similarities in the picture of government presented independent of the actual number of actors in the government or the means by which the executive has come to office. If the presidency is particularly constrained in the kind of symbolism that can be projected, one would expect (4) more similarities among presidents than between presidents and other contemporareous speakers. Finally, if the office is more religious than secular in its nature, one would expect (5) more similarities between presidents and religious speakers than between presidents and those in political and corporate fields.

A few answers to these questions have already been supplied. Roderick Hart compares speeches of presidents, presidential candidates, and religious and corporate leaders on several dimensions, including optimism, complexity, abstraction, and self-reference. He finds that presidents score highest among the speakers in optimism and are among the lowest in complexity and abstraction. They are most likely to engage in plain talk, but it is encouraging and optimistic plain talk. He also finds that presidents are more rhetorically similar to one another than they are to other leaders or to themselves before they become president. Self-references decline on assuming office and continue to decline through the course of the administration. Apparently a president "begins to feel that his will and the Nation's are isomorphic, that he has become America incarnate."[20] This same isomorphism, or symbolic equivalence, has been found for the modern presidents in this study. Hart concludes that "the office changes the person." The presidency is more than the president himself.[21]

These questions assume that presidents can be compared with others and that the individual in office is not unique. Consequently, people must get past their own socialization to answer them. Many writers on the presidency, along with the press and public, refer to *The President*: a singular term, used with the masculine pronoun. This is the Lonely Man in the White House, somehow set apart from all other people. This is also a part of the symbolic presidency as previous chapters have shown. If the person is unique, he cannot be compared to his counterparts in other executive offices or to his predecessors. Traditions can be lost, alternative forms of leadership disregarded, speeches copied from each other, and no one will know. The institution grows haphazardly while people insist that there is no institution—only an individual who governs. Use of the alternative form *presidents* could show the office more clearly and encourage much-needed comparisons. The Lonely Man in the White House is one among many in making symbolic presentations.

6

Beyond Reform

People, as Erving Goffman and others make clear, present themselves in ways to influence others. Presidents do so, too. Their choice of activities, words, and physical surroundings combine to create a picture of who they are and what they do in the government. But while it is commonly recognized that presidents make these symbolic projections, no sustained investigation has been made. The literature on the presidency has not investigated the symbolism directly, separating the study of rhetoric from that of the institution. The literature on symbolic politics indicates that a study of presidential symbolism is needed, but does not provide it beyond a few suggestive examples. This book attempts to extend both literatures to contribute to each other. By investigating the office of the modern presidency, it offers one systematic look at symbolism in a political institution.

Symbols can be considered as any set of words or actions conveying to an audience a range of meaning beyond themselves. They need not be factually true, but will invoke ideas and feelings people want to believe in as true. This book examines the symbolic presentation of the presidential office to see what pictures of government are conveyed. It focuses on the public actions of presidents, from Truman to Reagan, to see how presidents portray themselves and the government. It then compares these presentations with other descriptions of the office. While this remains a first investigation of the subject, a number of components do emerge clearly.

These components can be called the *symbolic presidency:* a particular set of expectations about the office that are held by the public, described by journalists and teachers, and encouraged by the presidents themselves. Together, they form a portrait of the presidency that can be recognized when it appears, traced across time, and distinguished from other portraits.

Seven Pictures of Government

Here, according to the modern presidents, is a capsule description.

1. The work of the government is carried on primarily by the president, the American people, and the nation. Together these three dominate the activity pictured, forming more than two-thirds of the sentence subjects and a large majority of all human references, in both major and minor addresses. While foreign policy speeches do show other nations and governments at work, the president remains the only American individual featured. The finding holds for the sample of State of the Union addresses selected and for the different audiences addressed.

2. These three government actors are actually one, linked by the word "we," and are indistinguishable from one another. The president equals the nation and equals the American people. This device is not merely the "royal we," used when a reference to "I" would be too awkward or personal. The word is used in several senses, often within the same argument and the same sentence. As the single most frequent subject of the sentence, the pronoun becomes the unifier of the entire action: The president speaks as the nation, to the nation, asking for the nation's support.

3. Presidents work alone in the government, with little help from Congress, administration officials, or other advisers. In the foreign policy speeches, ambassadors, cabinet secretaries, or joint chiefs are rarely mentioned. The same holds for economic speeches where key congressional committees, the Council of Economic Advisers, or other economists are noticeable for their absence. Interest-group audiences receive the same presentation, even though these groups would themselves be working firsthand with the many participants in government and would be very aware of their importance. Overall, Congress—or any congressional reference—forms 2 percent of the sentence subjects, while the executive branch references total 3 percent.

The government is not shown to have a separation of powers. When Congress is mentioned at all, it is trivialized and dismissed. Congress appears active primarily in planning or returning from its adjournment. It does not oppose the president—it merely goes home. It is true that members of Congress, unlike the president, are shown participating in the political process. They belong to political parties and run for election. However, Congress appears to be a very minor actor and part-time participant on the scene. The characterization holds equally for presidents of the same and opposing party as the party in control of Congress; and it holds for presidents, such as Johnson and Ford, who had previously spent long years as successful congressional leaders. The exceptional cases when presidents admit facing congressional opposition stand out by their very infrequency: Truman (former senator) once; Ford (a House leader) once; and Reagan (with no congressional experience) in two economic addresses.

4. Interest groups are a synonym for the American people. These groups too, are presented in ways quite far from the reality of American politics. When groups are mentioned at all, they are combined in such a way as to add up to the American people: the old and the young; wage earners and the unemployed; business, farmers, and labor. Almost without exception, groups are not shown as holding interests opposed to one another, even when the groups themselves are addressed. So Eisenhower, in all seriousness, compliments the AFL-CIO for being "apolitical." The American Medical Association can help the president guard the nation's spiritual health. Presidents, then, do not need to face conflict or reconcile different interests as part of their job in the White House. With the groups transformed into the American people, who in turn are one with the president, few cases of controversy remain.

5. Presidents do not engage in political or electoral activity. Parties and elections are mentioned only to be denied—as something presidents do not do—or as an activity Congress engages in. So, the past Republican leader of Congress, Gerald Ford, boasts that he is not identified with a political party; and Richard Nixon refers to his "good friends in the field of politics." In the major addresses references to God and religion far outnumber references to parties and elections, and in the minor speeches words such as *vote, election, ballot,* and *campaign* are heard only within the confines of the president's own party. No difference was found for the election-year speeches compared to those in the first three years of the term. In short, it could not be known from the presidents' accounts how they had come to office—whether through election, monarchical succession, or divine anointing. They say they are to be considered equivalent to the nation and the American people without providing the electoral basis for that assertion.

6. Presidents are the cultural and religious leaders of the nation. They lead prayers, quote from the Bible, and urge their congregation to look to matters of the spirit. Overall, references to religion far outnumber those to parties and elections, and even in the economic addresses, God is cited more frequently than the Federal Reserve or the Council of Economic Advisers. While many of the religious allusions bolster support for administration proposals, no line is drawn between public and private moral activity. Reagan says that inauguration days should be declared days of prayer; Carter says we must strengthen the American family, which is the basis of our society; and Nixon tells us to listen to "the better angels of our nature," to celebrate goodness, decency, and love.

Elsewhere, Kennedy urges us to fight "for the American dollar and for freedom" and Truman asks for a strong anti-inflation law so the country can fight for world peace.

The lack of boundaries is seen in the schedule of activities and the minor addresses as well. Presidents give a State of the Union message every January and a Christmas message every December. They light a national Christmas tree. They speak to foreign diplomats and religious leaders, to astronauts and football heroes in the same capacity as symbol of the nation and the government. They advance ideas on science, academic standards, American novelists, and art. Overall, more time is spent in the role of religious and cultural leader than is spent addressing parties and economic interest groups.

7. Presidents are unique, alone, without peers. Apart from the flag and the seal of office, presidents show themselves without companions or background detail. Place references are absent or limited to famous battlefields and other historical sites. The same abstraction and lack of detail is found in the setting in time. Presidents rarely speak about specific historical events or past administrations, mentioning only a few great presidents, the American Revolution, and successful wars. Ford makes an exception in his remarks on taking office and speaks of the Nixon resignation. Reagan discusses past economic policy. But beyond these exceptional cases, presidents give little sense that others have stood in the same place, said many of the same things, and faced the same problems before. Alone in the government and unique in time, presidents cannot be compared with their predecessors. They say that we will now go forward, we will—once again—begin. The "new" beginning is repeated by each president, often in the same words. The past is symbolically abolished with each inauguration, and the new president stands alone.

Perhaps most important, one finds a striking similarity in these pictures across time, circumstances, and political party. Through forty years of American history, presidents present themselves to the public in much the same way. They are alone in the government, equivalent to the nation, religious and cultural leaders who shun politics and elections. The similarity carries to details of characterization and specific devices used: The vacationing Congress and the citizen letter writers are two cases in point. Presidents explain the need for military action by photographs of military supplies, whether missile bases or warehouses piled with rifles or rice. They remind their audience that Americans are not aggressors and fight wars only for peace. They ask for a stronger moral fibre to support the economy and give the same picture of interest groups. Each kind of speech has its own recognizable character. The same details are included and left out.

Some variation occurs. On one occasion Ford finds it necessary to discuss elections and Reagan talks of negotiations with Congress. Kennedy is more likely to discuss foreign nations and Johnson domestic groups. Carter and Eisenhower are the most abstract; Nixon and Reagan are the most colloquial. While the Kennedy inaugural became famous for its style and particular rhetorical effect, that rhetoric is not found in other Kennedy speeches. Except for the minor stylistic differences, it would be difficult to tell the presidents and their speeches apart. Overall, the similarities are much more striking than the differences, holding across parties, diverse circumstances, and very different personal styles. In short, one finds an *institutionalized* portrayal of the office carried on through the public record created by the presidents themselves. An institution persists beyond the particular events and style of the individual in office. It is maintained over time and takes on a life of its own. Thus Kennedy and Reagan might disagree about the place of religion in government, but both present the president as a moral leader. Circumstances change, advisers rise and fall from favor, speechwriters come and go, but the same picture of the office is presented and carried on across time.

The minor addresses, in contrast, give more of a sense of individual style and preferences. While the office is shown in the same way, different groups are addressed from one president to another. One sees Truman's liking for the Masons, Nixon's for football, Kennedy's for gatherings with foreign diplomats in the White House. Johnson and Carter add visits with blacks and women's groups, whereas their successors in office do not. Johnson makes remarks in the White House each time a piece of Great Society legislation is passed while Nixon makes virtually no remarks, but addresses each government agency in turn. Ford speaks to party groups more frequently than other presidents do. Indeed, it may be the choices made in the minor remarks and scheduling arrangements that give much of the personality to an administration. But these differences make the similarity of the major addresses all the more striking.

These findings can be broadened to more general statements. The continuities suggest an institutionalized portrayal of the office carried on by the presidents themselves. The president is the single head of the government and moral leader of the nation who speaks for and may be taken as equivalent to all the people. He expresses thoughts and feelings to the nation and does not engage in politics, an unnecessary activity in any case, since there are no major competitive actors or controversy among interest groups. Other details of the portrayal are hazier. It is not clear how presidents came to office or what, besides expressing thoughts and feelings, they do in government.

The results show a convergence between presidents and others in this symbolic presentation. Presidents, say many academics and journalists in their writing, are

- Identical to the nation
- Identical to the government and the powers of government
- Unique and alone
- The moral leaders of the nation

Writing in 1976, after Watergate and the era of the imperial presidency, one presidential scholar offered the following description:

> [The president] will, by example, image, and appeal, try as best he can to lead in the ideals and traditions of the past, and be sensitive to national missions that lie ahead. He will try to unify the people around these national missions so as to realize the dreams of a way of life for the United States. . . . He will be President of *all* the people.
>
> He should be steeped in our national history and traditions. He will thereby recognize the elements of greatness in our greatest Presidents—Washington, Jefferson, Lincoln, the two Roosevelts, Wilson, and Truman.
>
> He should also recognize the conflicting, confusing, and dangerous elements in our contemporary society and the world at large—and the elements of promise. With deep understanding of all these, with a combination of determination and humility as God gives him to see the right, he will be the biggest man he can be, adding to his own strength the strength of others who like him would recapture a sense of mission for our people.[1]

The president is identified with the nation and "all the people." The past is represented by a few great presidents and the future holds a promise. Politics is not mentioned. The president is a moral leader closely associated with God, who will articulate and unify the people around a national mission. He is humble while trying to be "the biggest man he can be." Each component in the description, and the effect of the whole, sounds identical to a presidential address.

Journalists carry on the same idealization. The 1988 election, in the view of many, reached a new low in electoral politics. But the winner of this contest was suddenly transformed. The front page of the *New York Times* that carried the election results did not show the winner at a victory party, surrounded by friends and campaign workers. The *Times* showed George Bush in solemn shadows—alone with the flag and the seal of office. The election could be forgotten; a new president was born.

The public, too, wipes out the past, giving support to the office no matter what the past incumbents have done. Ford's support was as high in his early days in office as Nixon's was in his first days. The graph in Figure 6.1 tells the story: The new president's popularity returns close to the high point of the past inauguration regardless of the low point reached in the intervening years.

The more individuals are blamed for mistakes and scandals the less the office is touched. After the Iran-*contra* scandal, many thousand pages of testimony, final reports, and press summaries documented exactly what Oliver North and John Poindexter did, what Bill Casey said and when he said it. In the amount of pages of print available to the public, these autopsies must be second only to the Watergate writing. But all this detail helps keep the individuals separate from the office. People psychoanalyze Nixon, make jokes about Reagan's attention span, and typecast North as a wild man or cult hero. This ton of writing does more than "explain" an event—it locates, or buries, it in individual trivia. The particular circumstances, in all their idiosyncratic detail, can never be reproduced: hence confidence is shaken in one president but not in the presidency. The slate is wiped clean, and support can rise again, on the next Inauguration Day.

What emerges is a symbolic picture of the office that is sharply defined. Consistent in its details and repetition, it can be recognized when it occurs, analyzed for its impact, and compared against other presentations. Sharply at odds with many facts of American politics, it nevertheless has a life of its own. It is maintained as true by a number of commentators

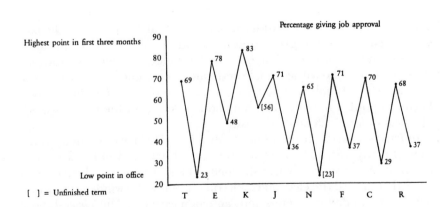

Figure 6.1
We Must Go Forward Now—the Highs and Lows of Presidential Popularity

over time and consistently adhered to by the presidents. Presidents and the public, journalists and academics—all help to shape the expectations of the office. There is no single agent or simple causal explanation. Rather, institutions are formed from the shared expectations of many people, reinforcing each other over time. Presidents shape the office, but they respond as well to the expectations of others. They are successful in fact, in winning elections or governing in the White House, in so far as they best embody what these expectations are.

A much earlier public opinion expert once told a political gathering, "I tell you that which you yourselves do know. (Shakespeare, *Julius Caesar*). Mark Anthony was aware, as he addressed the Roman populace at the death of Caesar, that the most effective leaders will appeal to what the public already believes or wants to be true. If the public thinks of presidents in a particular way, then presidents and others who address the public are well advised to follow these expectations. The result for the office is that the ideas continue over time, influencing future citizens and presidents.

This same dynamic allows change as well as continuity. Expectations can shift with circumstances or with conscious attention. They can also change through a process that is gradual and imperceptible, as the previous chapter showed. Memories grow indistinct across a two-term president's stay in office. Two such presidents (or one Franklin Roosevelt) and the ideas of an entire generation are affected. Traditions are dropped, lost, or given new definitions and the office is transformed.

Implications

The results point also to wider implications for those who describe the office and teach about it. A set of symbolic components have been identified quite far from the facts of American government. Presidents, in fact, are not the single head of the government. As individuals, they may not even be aware of, much less control, many of the decisions taken in their name. They do not inherit a blank slate whereby all things are possible and everything is made new. Policies and problems continue over several administrations; bureaucrats and members of Congress remain at work as presidents come and go. Groups are active and in competition with one another for the allocations of government. Presidents represent one political party and a set of constituencies with closer ties to some groups than others. They are selected through a process of nomination and election that does not encourage humility or altruism, but does demand the ability to manipulate symbols and the most sharply honed political skills. Overall, things are not the way them seem. When presidents act most powerfully, they are least likely to claim themselves synonymous with the power of the nation. The presidents who appear most religious in private life are not the symbolic religious leaders. Claims of vision and innovation are given in copied formulas showing a poverty of language and imagination. Speeches urging the nation forward limit themselves to memories of the past.

It is the magic of symbolism to create illusion. But illusion has costs that must be considered by journalists, teachers of politics, and future presidents. Is the nation best served by carrying on the symbolism or by challenging it? Should the two contradictory pictures, in a kind of schizophrenic fashion, be carried on together? If so, what line should be drawn and what accommodation made between the two?

The questions are compounded by the peculiar openness of the office to changing interpretations. By definition, all institutions are shaped by the expectations of relevant actors. The presidency is particularly susceptible to such influence. It was to have sufficient vigor and energy, in the words of Alexander Hamilton, to do what needed to be done for the needs of the developing nation. It could grow and develop with changing historical circumstances and become what people wanted it to be. But this means that those who describe the office, and so shape the expectations of others, need to think seriously about what they are doing. Statements of fact, whether correct or incorrect, become the very real building blocks for the office of the future. Early in the twentieth century, presidents and others said that the American chief executive should play the role of world leader, and the office has come to include that role. If presidents and others now say that the American chief executive should be a cultural and religious leader, than that component too may become institutionalized, shaping future ideas about what presidents should do.

How, then, should people describe this office and present it to others? Four major arguments can be made.

First, some would say that intellectual honesty permits only one answer. If a statement is incorrect, no matter how popular, then it needs to be challenged with the best information available. The world may not be flat and the president may not have very much control over, or even understand, the programs put forward in his name. Critics and teachers of politics must attempt to stand apart from their own society and its current fashions and indeed have a responsibility to do so. Therefore, if the current picture of the presidency is incorrect or out of focus, then these people should be the ones to correct it. Further, if symbolism is so central to the office, then the symbolism itself should be made explicit. It needs to be identified, talked about, and watched for its effects on the government.

The public, too, needs this clarification. Basic to democratic thinking is the idea of an informed citizenry. Hence people need to be able to assign separate responsibility to the president and Congress, to compare presidents one to another, to see a White House proposal apart from its patriotic and moral decorations. Americans do in fact assume that they can judge their presidents. They rate the "job" being done in Washington, explain why they like one candidate better than another, and rank past presidents from great to mediocre. Since people make these judgments anyway, and feel that they should do so as citizens, they need the most accurate information possible.

Second, others would say that the current information is good enough. People cope with symbolism and internal contradictions in all aspects of life and can do so with the presidency. So, while Ronald Reagan called the Nicaraguan *contras* "freedom fighters" and announced "I am a *contra*," a majority of the public disapproved of the president's *contra* aid proposal. Symbolism can be accepted at one level of consciousness and questioned at another level. In short, the public is not so easily fooled. People can know the emperor is wearing no clothes—and still enjoy the parade.

Third, others would argue that these pictures, whether accurate or not, have harmful effects on the government. They can undermine key constitutional principles, reduce public participation, and do damage to the office itself. We say we have "a government of laws and not of men." But this principle means that no individual is above the law or should be exalted over it. So, when presidents cast themselves as equivalent to the nation and Richard Neustadt writes "what is good for the president is good for the nation,"[2] that constitutional principle is directly challenged. During the Watergate hearings in 1974, one White House witness after another justified wrongdoing on the grounds that reelecting Richard Nixon was the most important thing that could be done for the country at the time. One such witness was a former attorney general, John Mitchell, the chief law-enforcement officer of the federal government. Evidently these people* had not heard of that constitutional principle. If what is good for the president is by definition good for the nation, then we have a government of men and not of laws.

The principle of checks and balances is challenged if the president is seen as the single head of government while Congress vacations or runs for reelection. A separation of church and state is also challenged if presidents explain the Deity's views on foreign policy, lead the nation in observing some religious holidays, and tell the people what is good. If government is what people say it is, then those principles become merely historical curiosities, rarely heard in the present day.

Moreover, exaggerated claims invite disillusionment and do damage to the office itself. When presidents cannot set all things right, they— and the government they are a symbol of—suffer a loss of support from the citizens. If no conflict exists between parties and among interest groups, why cannot the president get more done? If Congress is not opposing the president when it does not pass legislation, what is it doing with all of its time? One student of the presidency identifies a self-defeating dynamic that "by inducing presidents to attempt to control all issues . . . leaves them in effective control of none."[3] Another suggests that "a more . . . critical approach to the presidency would not only prepare our young with a more objective understanding of politics, leadership, and civil participation; it could also contribute to a more effective and healthy presidency."[4] Given unrealistic hopes, disillusionment is inevitable. Presidential popularity, measured by public opinion polls, falls throughout the term from the high point on inauguration day. Since the president cannot save the country from a host of assorted ills, the polls drop as the ills continue and unrealistic expectations are not met. By this argument, a less grandiose view of the office might lead to more, rather than less, support for presidents and the government.

Fourth, others would say that the presentation helps provide much-needed power for the office. "Symbolic power," as Michael Novak and others argue, may be "the precondition of pragmatic power."[5] If the office is shaped by the expectations of others, then reduced expectations would limit the president even further. Congress may hesitate to oppose presidents on matters of controversy primarily because of the symbolic aura surrounding the office. Invitations to the White House, special briefings in a room that is itself a historical monument, plus the fact that it is the *president* who is asking the member's help—all provide powerful emotional persuasion. If members of Congress expect the president to be "as big . . . as he can be," and know the public has the same idea, they may act one way in legislative bargaining, whereas if they are reminded of the limits of the office, they may act quite differently. Reduced expectations can affect public opinion too. People may respect individual presidents more for what they are attempting to do, but think less of, and give less support to, the office.

In the past, many writers on the presidency consciously took this position. Presidents alone were capable of solving the nation's problems and so must be given more power (and more support in the American government textbooks) to enable them to do so. Consequently, these writers argued for a more powerful presidency and at the same time described the office in terms of this more powerful ideal. Hence the textbook presidency—unique and larger than life. For these writers, presenting the office more realistically and less grandly would hurt the nation, undercutting what little power presidents have.

Just as clearly, the office could be harmed by making the symbolism explicit. Presidential scholar Clinton Rossiter concludes a chapter on the history of the presidency:

And who, then, can measure the strength that is given to the President because he holds Lincoln's office, lives in Lincoln's house, and walks in Lincoln's way? The final greatness of the Presidency lies in the truth that it is not just an office of incredible power but a breeding ground of indestructible myth.[6]

Rossiter recounts the history of great presidents only; therefore, he is carrying on the myth at the same time he discusses it. But if these mythic components are fundamental to the greatness of the office, they may not bear too much conscious examination. Myths probably are not as indestructible as Rossiter suggests. Indeed, they may be particularly vulnerable when labeled as myths.

So is it useful to point out that Lincoln's house has seen its share of scandals, too? That presidents can tell lies and that the lights will burn in the White House, even though the president is sleeping? What damage is done to the office by challenging the myths about it?

There is a surface attraction to the last argument that might not stand up to closer scrutiny. Ironically, when presidents do have power in their own hands—to grant a pardon, fire a general, or call state troops into federal service—they do not make these symbolic statements. They say in a matter of fact way, without biblical quotes or other flourishes, what they as individual will do. The symbolism is an expression of the weakness of the presidency and not of its power. It is also hard to make the case that the symbolism helps the president's power to persuade. Speeches do not in fact produce a rise in public support, an earlier chapter showed. At most, the action of giving a speech, independent of its rhetorical content, seemed to slow the inevitable decline at the polls. The few speeches that deviated from the usual symbolism showed no difference in impact from the other speeches. Congress, too, appeared unmoved by the particulats of presidential rhetoric. Reagan was no less successful when he talked about party politics than when he followed the usual practice and made no reference to parties. Ford had trouble with Congress whether he said its members were vacationing or called it the coequal branch.

Another irony is discovered. Advocates of the symbolic presidency ask the occupants of the office to have vision, to be innovators, to lead the nation forward. The presidents say they are doing this in all of their public presentations. However, the new roads chosen are the old roads; the words and visions are copies from the past. The earlier twentieth century presidents showed a variety in their choice of symbols: some emphasized religion while others did not; some talked about party platforms or what they as individuals would do. The contemporary presidents show no such variety. The current symbolism is a substitute for innovation—it encourages presidents to follow—and recycle—the speeches of the past. Making the symbolism explicit should not only hold presidents more accountable for what they are trying to do, it should also challenge them to do more.

Few would say that presidents should divest themselves of all symbolic support or that extreme frankness is a virtue in office. But what balance should be drawn between symbol and substance, and which symbolic statements are the important ones? A set of particular components have been identified, some of which may be more useful or threatening to the nation than others are. Should the public be made more aware of checks and balances or of awesome presidential power? Should people be reminded about a government of laws or shown that the president equals the nation? Should they be taught that the two principles are mutually contradictory? What proportion of a president's time should be spent on cultural and religious occasions? If presidents can rally the nation to new achievements and goals, are there boundaries to what they should be rallying it to see?

All this is not to exaggerate the impact of political scientists or to underestimate the power of a public philosophy. It is not at all apparent that many journalists and academics want to change the office. The news media, themselves attuned to the power of illusion, speak well of other practitioners of the craft. During the first months of George Bush's presidency, the press critized the lack of "vision" in his speeches, the absence of a clear sense of direction in his leadership, and his low public profile. A *New York Times* editorial of May 25, 1989 described a Bush foreign policy speech as "flat and flimsy," calling on him to recognize "the power of language and bold goals." The American president was being eclipsed by a Russian leader who could even rival Ronald Reagan as a television personality. During the same year, a leading political theorist argued that American presidential leadership is essentially patriarchal, or prophetic, in the biblical tradition. Citing the same *Times* editorial, H. Mark Roelofs showed how presidents are called to expand the religious character of the office to "congregate" the nation. Like Moses, the American leaders are asked to show that they are blessed, identify themselves and the people together in a shared history, and personally show the people a way forward into the future.[7] It may well be that the expectations that have created the symbolic presidency are too powerful to be turned aside.

Still, if pictures of the office do shape how it is perceived and therefore what it becomes, further thinking on these questions is important. Journalists have discussed how much they contribute to the making of news by their reporting of it. Individual political scientists, too, must decide for themselves the line to be drawn between the teaching of government and the contributing to it. At minimum, people might become more aware and critical of the symbolism occurring around them. Moses led a people already "congregated"—by a common religion, kinship ties, and a shared historical experience. His verbal attempts to enforce compliance had to be buttressed repeatedly by terrifying displays of divine intervention. If American presidents are held to a Mosaic ideal, they will be either doomed to fail or forced to change the basic structure of the government. The ideal modern president, according to the standards Roelofs identifies as operative in the American political system, may have been the Ayatollah.

Beyond Reform

The results pose wider implications for the office and the various reform proposals that are so commonly heard. Writers from Woodrow Wilson to Richard Neustadt argued that presidents were not strong enough to fulfill the demands of leadership expected of them. Coming fresh from the people with a new electoral mandate, presidents would find their programs blocked by a little band of committee members—or Supreme Court justices—who had come to office long before. Nor could they trust the loyalty of executive branch personnel to do what they wanted done. Orders, Neustadt observed, might not be carried out. A president could say, "Do this" or "Do that," and nothing would happen. Consequently, reformers in the 1940s and 1960s sought ways to increase the power of the office compared to the other branches. In the 1970s, in contrast, reformers tried to limit the office and make it more accountable. Presidents were too strong. Arthur Schlesinger and others spoke of the "imperial presidency," arguing that reforms were needed to check executive excesses. Congress, for example, should be strengthened in budget making, foreign policy, and oversight to provide checks on presidential power.

Other reforms focused on organizing the White House. In the 1950s writers called attention to the impossible burden of the office and announced that "the President needs help." They urged an expanded White House staff, with people personally loyal to the president, and improved organizational machinery. In the wake of Watergate and Vietnam, the new machinery itself became the subject of criticism. Alexander George, Irving Janis, and others called for improvements in the quality, rather than the quantity, of White House decision making.[8] The advisers might be too loyal, too eager for consensus, too concerned with keeping the president's favor. The help itself, and the kind of biases it introduced, became the problem. The selection process, too, has been a perennial target for reform. People have worried about the packaging of the president by public relations firms and the effects of media reporting in primaries and elections. Party nominating procedures were reformed, with writers then debating how the reforms themselves needed reforming.

But reforms based on an unrealistic view of the office will not be that helpful or feasible. In the first place, *some of the problems may not actually exist—they may be artifacts of false perceptions.* Take the idea that presidents work alone in the government, without help from Congress, advisers, or the experience of past administrations. They are the single head of the government, leader of the free world, and cultural and religious leader of the nation. If one focuses on this picture—of the impossible job of the lonely man in the White House—then presidents definitely do need more help. But if they do not work alone or deal with more than a small fraction of the work of government, the problem looks less severe. Indeed, they may have more protection from the typical time-consuming cares of the day than most other executives and busy people. Past presidential adviser George Reedy has described the support system of the White House as designed to cater to the president's every whim. Reedy's firsthand observation is that presidents are less busy than they are made to appear. "There is far less to the presidency," he remarks, "in terms of essential activity, than meets the eye." He admits that the psychological burdens are immense, but adds that "no president ever died of overwork."[9] It is true that the president must address the Boy Scouts, Future Farmers of America, and many other groups, at the rate of one event for nearly every working day. But this particular burden of the office is not what the reformers have in mind.

More basically, false expectations can lead to calls for reform where none is needed. If presidents are expected to produce economic prosperity, solve all social problems, and unite the nation, then the failure to do so suggests something is wrong. They need more power, or more help, or something, to bring results closer to expectations. But in the real political world where controversy, complex events, and unreconcilable points of view permit no ultimate solutions, the office may be functioning as well as possible. If presidents are not a universal providence that can set all things right, no reforms of the office can make them do so.

Second, *some of the problems may be caused by the unrealistic perceptions.* Reedy argues that the atmosphere surrounding the White House isolates presidents from political reality and obscures their judgment: "[The president] is treated with all the reverence due a monarch. . . . No one speaks to him unless spoken to first. No one ever invites him to 'go soak your head' when his demands become petulant and unreasonable."[10] But few would want to tell the nation or the American people to go soak their heads, and few would charge the leader of the nation's morality with being petulant. Further if presidents must engage in the kind of thinking that carries on two contradictory realities at once, this too can impair the judgments taken in the White House, while exacting other psychic costs. By this argument, changing the structure of White House advising will not change the quality of its decisions. One would need to change the perceptions of the presidents and their advisers.

During the Iran-*contra* hearings, several witnesses blamed Congress for the illegal actions carried on in the White House. If Congress had not interfered with the president's role as foreign policymaker, then such extreme measures would not have been necessary. This sounds analogous to the car thief blaming the owner for leaving the keys in the ignition. However, if Congress is only a trivial participant in government, that kind of argument makes sense. If only one individual makes policy for the nation, a congressional law becomes interference with that role. Presidents are expected to make foreign policy alone. Since constitutionally they cannot do so, they are forced to go outside the constitution to fulfill the expectations.[11]

Many writers point out the disturbing tendency of symbolism over substance in government. They see presidents encouraged to lie, fake, and mislead others, and to be so preoccupied with symbol manipulation and information control that they do not have time for other activities.[12] But it should not be surprising that presidents are packaged in election campaigns, that media commentary can make or break candidates, or that symbol takes precedence over substance. Nor should it be surprising that ceremonial and religious occasions outnumber the governmental and international in the minor addresses—that indeed much of the burden of the office comes from these ceremonial demands. Candidates are selected who can best perform the duties of the office and the duties are to make these symbolic projections. Hence, if people would like an office of more substance and less appearance, reforms must come from changing the perceptions.

Can presidents lie and present misleading information to the American people? Why, they are encouraged to do so in every public presentation they make. And why should they need to do so? Because the job they are expected to do is so at odds with the job they can actually do. So, again if people want fewer coverups, secret arms deals, or other dishonesties in the White House, they must ask for a more fundamental honesty in presenting the office.

Finally, *the perceptions may obscure problems that do exist.* Reforms cannot be made if they are not identified. If presidents automatically become the sum of all American virtues, one does not need to examine the selection process that carefully. Either the process is fine or the office itself—"Lincoln's office . . . Lincoln's house"—automatically transforms ordinary human beings into something much finer. We need not worry how vice-presidents are selected or how the advisers are chosen who make decisions in the president's name. But if these people share the normal range of human vices, and no magic transformation occurs in the White House, then the selection needs closer attention. Could American presidents be dishonest and yet give the illusion of honesty? Could they be self-absorbed while seeming compassionate, or power-hungry while appearing humble? If this is so, can the selection process sort fact from illusion? Are there changes in media coverage, primaries, or campaign activities that could help distinguish one from the other?

Who are the aides chosen as personally loyal to the president and what kind of traits can they be expected to have? They set priorities, make the calls that come from the White House, and decide what will or will not reach the president's attention. What are their qualifications and experience for the job? Aides tend to be personal friends and campaign workers from before the election. Could the public learn more about these potential White House decision makers before the election? Once in office, can these advisers be made more accountable without sacrificing the loyalty and discretion that presidents need? Since presidents do not work alone in government, those that work with them may need to be held accountable too.

One-third of American vice-presidents have gone on to become president—more than one-third in the twentieth century. Others, Spiro Agnew, for example, automatically became leading contenders for a future presidential race by virtue of their vice-presidential nomination. Dan Quayle may well be such a contender in 1996. While some vice-presidents had extensive experience in government, others did not. Some were scarcely known by the presidential candidates. Nevertheless, these individuals inherit the same exalted expectations that other presidents do and, according to earlier chapters, act in the same way. Four of the presidents examined—Truman, Johnson, Nixon, Ford—came to the office after serving as vice-president. Four—Eisenhower, Kennedy, Carter, Reagan—did not. No differences are seen between the two groups of presidents, with the exception of Ford's remarks on not being elected. The former vice-presidents identify with the nation and the American people, take the role of moral leader, and set cultural priorities. It is a strength of the vice-presidency, of course, to provide an automatic transferral of power at a president's death. The vice-president becomes president with all of the responsibilities and duties of the office. Still, if presidents can possess the full range of human vices, these often-little-known vice-presidents can, too. If nothing magical happens when a person becomes president, then people might need to look more closely at these candidates and think how they might best be selected.

If presidents are not unique, could we use the experience of past presidents, now forced to maintain an awkward retirement with only the occasional honorary degree or conference with foreign leaders to occupy their time? No one, it is said, can prepare for the presidency. But these individuals have prepared—and have the results of their experience to offer. Writers point out a paradox of experience and influence in the White House. Presidents lose support the longer they are in office; hence those least experienced in making White House decisions are the most likely to succeed.[13] When everything is made new, it is also made inexperienced. This is not to argue for a plural presidency—there is only one president in office at any one time. But if the past could be acknowledged, even marginally, it might be used to improve the quality of government.

One of George Washington's choices has not been followed by many of his successors; the tradition of giving a Farewell Address along with advice and warnings for the future. Washington offered "disinterested warnings of a parting friend, who can possibly have no personal motive to bias his counsel." Many people have heard of his counsel against the danger of party, but few know of his more ominous warning against geographic divisions of the union. He also gave advice on foreign policy and one last plea for a strong central government. Eisenhower followed Washington's tradition, warning of the dangers of a military-industrial complex that the general and skilled politician had come to know well. Carter, too, gave a Farewell Address, cautioning his audience not to let times of threat and complicated issues overrun the rights of citizens. These rights, Carter said, are not the salt on the bread, but the bread itself. In each of these cases, presidents used their unique position and outlook to raise a warning that might not otherwise be heard. Of all the presidential addresses, these might be the most important to hear.

Presidents identify themselves with only a few great moments in American history. The rest of the past is abolished with each new administration. But do presidents come to the office of Washington and Lincoln only, or the office of Grant, Harding, and Nixon too? If scandals and abuses of power cold occur in the past, why should we be surprised when they occur again? No changes have been made that suggest they could not occur. Or occur again in another ten years. Watergate was seen as a problem of Nixon and his advisers, the fault traced to the individual in office at the time. The Iran-*contra* affair, too, was seen as a problem with people who assumed too much power and a president who was not in control. Ten years from now there will be other special circumstances to explain the next set of revelations. This does not absolve the individuals from blame. It does suggest, however, that individual explanations are not sufficient. Just like the presidents, we abolish the past and the mistakes of the past. We put Watergate behind us. We put Irangate behind us. And the next president will enter the office of Washington and Lincoln and say Let us begin.

The fundamental question for reformers and others is the matter of definition. The office is open to become what people say it is and expect it to be. Americans, then, need to think more carefully about the kind of presidency they want, since they will probably get the one they ask for.

Appendix A:
Major Presidential Addresses, Truman to Reagan, First Three Years of Term

Truman

State of the Union, 5 January 1949
Inaugural Address, 20 January 1949
Economic Policy, 13 July 1949
State of the Union, 4 January 1950
Korean War, 19 July 1950
Korean War, 1 September 1950
Defense Production Act, 9 September 1950
National Emergency-Korean War, 15 December 1950
State of the Union, 8 January 1951
Korean War/MacArthur, 11 April 1951
Inflation Controls, 14 June 1951
International Arms Reduction, 7 November 1951

Eisenhower

Inaugural Address, 20 January 1953
State of the Union, 2 February 1953
World Peace, 16 April 1953
National Security, 19 May 1953
Cabinet, 3 June 1953
Korean Armistice, 26 July 1953
Achievements of the Administration and the 83rd Congress, 6 August 1953
Achievements of the Administration, 4 January 1954
State of the Union, 7 January 1954
Tax Program, 15 March 1954
National Goals and Problems, 5 April 1954
Achievements of the 83rd Congress, 23 August 1954
State of the Union, 6 January 1955

Major addresses are defined as inaugural addresses, speeches before joint sessions of Congress, and speeches to the nation, broadcast nationwide on television. The key words preceding the date of the speech are taken from the title of the speech as printed in *The Public Papers of the Presidents*.

Geneva Conference, 15 July 1955
Geneva Conference, 25 July 1955

Kennedy

Inaugural Address, 20 January 1961
State of the Union, 30 January 1961
National Problems, 25 May 1961
European Trip, 6 June 1961
Berlin Crisis, 25 July 1961
State of the Union, 11 January 1962
Nuclear Disarmament, 2 March 1962
Economic Policy, 13 August 1962
University of Mississippi, 30 September 1962
Cuban Missile Crisis, 22 October 1962
State of the Union, 14 January 1963
Racial Strife in Birmingham, 12 May 1963
Civil Rights, 11 June 1963
Nuclear Test Ban Treaty, 26 July 1963
Nuclear Test Ban and Tax Reduction, 18 September 1963

Johnson

State of the Union, 4 January 1965
Inaugural Address, 20 January 1965
Voting Rights, 15 March 1965
Dominican Republic, 2 May 1965
Steel Industry, 30 August 1965
Steel Settlement, 3 September 1965
State of the Union, 12 January 1966
State of the Union, 10 January 1967
Detroit Riot, 24 July 1967
Civil Disorder, 27 July 1967
Vietnam War, 29 September 1967

Nixon

Inaugural Address, 20 January 1969
Vietnam War, 14 May 1969
Domestic Programs, 8 August 1969
Vietnam War, 3 November 1969
Vietnam War, 15 December 1969
State of the Union, 22 January 1970
Vietnam War, 20 April 1970
Cambodian Invasion, 30 April 1970
Cambodian Invasion, 3 June 1970
Economic Policy, 17 June 1970
Peace Initiatives in Vietnam, 7 October 1970
State of the Union, 22 January 1971
Vietnam War, 7 April 1971

Economic Policy, 15 August 1971
Economic Policy, 9 September 1971
Economic Policy, 7 October 1971
Supreme Court Nominations, 21 October 1971

Ford

Remarks on Taking Oath of Office, 9 August 1974
Address to Joint Session of Congress, 12 August 1974
Nixon Pardon, 8 September 1974
Economic Policy, 8 October 1974
Energy and the Economy, 13 January 1975
State of the Union, 15 January 1975
Tax Reduction Bill, 29 March 1975
U.S. Foreign Policy, 10 April 1975
Energy Policy, 27 May 1975
Federal Tax and Spending Reductions, 6 October 1975

Carter

Inaugural Address, 20 January 1977
Report to the American People, 2 February 1977
Energy Policy, 18 April 1977
Energy Policy, 20 April 1977
Energy Policy, 8 November 1977
State of the Union, 19 January 1978
Panama Canal Treaties, 1 February 1978
Camp David Summit, 18 September 1978
Economic Policy, 24 October 1978
State of the Union, 23 January 1979
Energy Policy, 5 April 1979
Vienna Summit and Salt II, 18 June 1979
National Goals, 15 July 1979
Soviets and Salt II, 1 October 1979

Reagan

Inaugural Address, 20 January 1981
Economic Policy, 5 February 1981
Economic Policy, 18 February 1981
Economic Policy, 28 April 1981
Tax Reduction, 27 July 1981
Economic Policy, 24 September 1981
State of the Union, 26 January 1982
Federal Budget, 29 April 1982
Tax and Budget Policy, 16 August 1982
Middle East, 1 September 1982
Lebanon, 20 September 1982
Economic Policy, 13 October 1982
Arms Reduction and Deterrence, 22 November 1982

State of the Union, 25 January 1983
National Security Policy, 23 March 1983
Central America, 27 April 1983
Soviet Attack on Airliner, 5 September 1983
Lebanon and Grenada, 27 October 1983

Appendix B:
Coding Rules

Each speech was coded by two coders. Intercoder reliability was obtained with 90 percent agreement or better reached for all pairs of coders. Identification of the sentence unit of analysis and the sentence subject was established in all cases by the author.

Coders were given the following definitions:

The Actors

The subject of the sentence is coded for all human actors (people, groups of people, nations, or institutions). Rhetorical expressions ("some might say") are not coded. The first subject only of compound sentences or sentences with compound subjects is counted.

The following categories are shown in table 2.1:

01 I, this administration, any personal reference (as "your president").

02 The nation, United States, this country, or synonym

03 the American people, Americans, each citizen, or synonym, referring to all the people and no specific groups. Thus "those Americans who fought. . .the wilderness" would be coded as 05 and then as 09.

04 The pronoun "we," when the context makes clear it refers to 01, 02, or 03.

05 All other actors (includes 07-12). The word "we" is coded here when the pronoun does not refer to 01, 02 or 03. For example, "we of the free world," "we in the Western Hemisphere."

The following categories are shown in table 2.3:

06 Combines coded items for 01-04.

07 Congress, any congressional reference, including House, Senate, congressional leaders, individual members, or committees, or synonyms (as Reagan's "Gang of 17").

08 Executive branch, advisers; includes all references to any executive agency or member, formal or informal presidential advisers, or references to "the government" or "government."

09 Subnational groups, American only; includes broad classifications (farmers, soldiers, the unemployed), as well as specific groups.

10 Other nations, governments, peoples; includes leaders of other nations or groups, revolutionary or military forces; also includes regions of the world or groups of people in more than one nation ("the Free World," "freedom-loving people everywhere").

11 Humanity, the world, or synonym.

12 A residual category used for all other human references; typical cases include references to famous people in history or citizen letter writers to presidents.

References to Parties and Elections

The following words, their plurals, and any other cognate forms are coded:

> Aisle, ballot, campaign, candidate (a candidate's name), convention (or city in which a convention was held), Democrat, elect, election, electoral process, lose (an election), majority, nominate, nomination, November (as reference to an election), opposition, party, partisan, partisanship, political, politician, politics, reelect, reelection, Republican, term (as one-term president), victory, vote, voters, win (an election), (year in which an election was held).

Religious References

The following words, their plurals, and any other cognate forms are coded. A phrase indicates that the entire phrase is coded as one word. A biblical quotation is also coded as one word.
All the words below actually appeared in the speeches.

Amen, angel, beacon, Bible, biblical (book of the Bible, quotation from the Bible), bless, blessed, blessing, brotherly love, cathedral, chalice, charity, Christmas, church, compassion, conscience, consecrate, covenant, crosses, curse, darkness, dark powers, dedicate (in context), devotion (in context), eternal, evil, faith, faithful, God (and synonyms as Creator, Almighty, Divine Power, and pronouns), golden rule, holy, humility, inner (in context), laws (as divine laws), light (in context), mercy, millennium, miracle, mission, oath, pilgrimage, pray, prayer, preach, righteous, righteousness, sacrament, sacred, sacrifice (as death), sanctity, shrine, soul, spirit (in context), spiritual, spirituality, star of David, summons, triumph in the right, trumpet, valley (in context), vow, wicked, worship.

Moral References

All moral references were read and coded in context. If the context appeared ambiguous, the word was included on the grounds that the ambiguity was probably intended. However, references to political values, such as *justice, freedom, peace,* are not included, nor are clear economic references, such as *responsible spending* or *economic principles.* Since context was interpreted generously to include ambiguous words, the number of moral words selected was limited more strictly. There are two clusters of moral references: a goodness cluster and an obligation cluster.

GOODNESS: character, courage (moral), decent, decency, dignity, false, fault, generous, good, good will, goodness, heal, healing, health, hero (for Reagan), honorably, humane, moral, morality, noble, nobility, principle, right, selfish, sick, standards, strength (as moral strength), true (in a moral sense), unselfish, value, whole (in a moral sense), wrong.

OBLIGATION: admonition, bind, bond, burden, cause, discipline, duty, earn, irresponsible, obligation, owe, required (as duty), responsible, responsibility, trust (as to keep a trust), worthy.

Appendix C:
Classification of Minor Addresses

Minor addresses are classified by audience and subject in terms of the following coding scheme. For results of the classification, see table 4.1 and discussion.

01 National Government

All remarks on signing bills and making appointments or nominations; all remarks to Congress, members of Congress, government agencies, or other national government personnel; any remarks on specific government policies (e.g., Vietnam amnesty) as opposed to general discussions (foreign affairs), which would be coded by audience into the appropriate category below.

02 International Affairs

All remarks abroad, except those addressed to U.S. citizens such as journalists or military personnel; all remarks in the United States addressed to representatives of foreign nations; all remarks to international organizations or those that cross national lines, except the religious organizations coded in 05.

03 Party Groups

All remarks to groups of either of the two major political parties.

04 Economic Interest Groups

All remarks to groups that seek material benefits from the federal government for their members, whether the group is broad or specific and whether the members must formally join or not; for example, farm, labor, and business groups; groups concerned with blacks, women, veterans, the handicapped; a chamber of commerce, the American Medical Association; all remarks to conferences of governors or mayors or other conferences of state or local officials.

05 Cultural and Religious Affairs

All remarks to religious gatherings or representatives of religious organizations; remarks to groups concerned with cultural or educational issues, with the exception of the economic interest groups coded above: thus, science, arts, journalism, entertainment, sports, citizenship; remarks to all youth organizations, university commencements, fraternal organizations; remarks on cultural and religious holidays.

06 Regional Travel

Remarks outside Washington, D.C., and not coded above: for example, speeches at airports on trips around the country; remarks at local ceremonies. Nixon's briefings on domestic policy to various regional media are included here, as well as Ford's "Conferences on Domestic and Economic Affairs," held in California, Florida, New Hampshire, and Ohio.

07 Ceremonial and Patriotic Affairs

Ceremonial remarks to military academies and military personnel (e.g., Medal of Honor recipients); ceremonies honoring other national figures past and present; other ceremonies and dedications within Washington, D.C.; remarks on patriotic holidays; remarks to patriotic groups. Ceremonies for government figures or interest-group representatives (a birthday party for a congressman, the dedications of a square in memory of Samuel Gompers) would be coded here rather than in categories 01 and 04, respectively.

08 Other

The residual category for remarks not coded above: primarily, talks on issues such as traffic safety, crime, conservation, not connected with a specific government policy or directed to an economic interest group.

Appendix D

Selected Listing from
The Public Papers—
April, Third Year of Term

Name, Date	Page(s)	Topic	Location and Time
TRUMAN, 1951			
April 2	209	Statement on the Third Anniversary of the European Recovery Program	
2	209–10	Toasts at a Dinner for Foreign Ministers of the Pan American Union	
*3	210–13	Address at the Cornerstone Laying of a Presbyterian Church	3:15 p.m.
3	213–14	Statement on the Second Anniversary of the North Atlantic Treaty	
5	214–17	The President's News Conference	Executive Office Bldg., 10:30 a.m.
5	217–18	Statement on Senate Resolution 99	
5	218	Statement on the Voice of America	
6	218–19	Letter to the President of the Red Cross on the Fund Campaign	
6	219–20	Letter to the Economic Stabilization Administrator on the Transportation Industry	

Includes all entries from the *Public Papers'* indexes, available from Truman through Reagan, for April of the third year of the term. For the one exception, proclamations and nominations, recorded only for the Carter and Reagan years, are excluded. The missing page numbers will indicate these excluded entries. The month was randomly selected from the first three years, excluding the first six months of an administration (approximately the honeymoon period), and the two months preceding the off-year congressional elections. An asterisk indicates a message delivered in person by the president, whether a major or minor address. Entries not receiving an asterisk include all written messages, exchanges such as interviews, toasts, or question-and-answer periods, and all indirect transcriptions.

15	533–34	Message to Congress on the Plan for U.S. Participation in the World Weather Program	
16	534–51	Interview at the Annual Convention of the American Society of Newspaper Editors	
*19	551–58	Remarks at the Republican Governors Conference in Williamsburg, Virginia	Conference Center, 11:26 a.m.
19	558–59	Message to Congress on the District of Columbia Budget	
*19	559–64	Remarks at the Convention of the Daughters of the American Revolution	Constitution, Hall, 9:30 p.m.
21	564–78	Message to Congress on Reform of the Foreign Assistance Program	
21	578–80	Message to the Senate Transmitting a Treaty on the U.S.-Mexico Boundary	
21	580–81	Memorandum about Women in Government	
*26	581–87	Remarks at a Meeting of the U.S. Chamber of Commerce	Constitution Hall, 11:10 a.m.
28	587–90	Statement on Proposals to Establish New National Wilderness Areas	
28	590–92	The President's News Conference	East Room, 9:00 p.m.
*30	602–4	Remarks Awarding a Citation to a Marine Division, Camp Pendleton, California	Parade Grounds, 12:32 p.m.

*FORD—
NO THIRD YEAR*

*CARTER,
1979*

April *1	578–79	Remarks to Reporters Concerning Three Mile Island Visit	Middletown, Pa., 3:00 p.m.
2	581–87	Message to Congress on Proposals to Protect the Privacy of Individuals	
2	587–90	Message to Congress Reporting on Recommendations of the National Commission for the Review of Federal and State Laws	
2	590–91	Letter to Six Congressional Committee Chairmen on Legislation to Implement the Egyptian-Israeli Peace Treaty	
2	591–98	Message to Congress Concerning the	

Legislation concerning the Department of
Education

*21	565	Remarks Following Meeting with President Gaston Thorn of the European Commission	White House, 11:40 a.m.
*21	568–72	Remarks and Question-and-Answer Session on Domestic and Foreign Policy Issues	White House, 1:34 p.m.
*22	572–73	Remarks at Swearing-in Ceremony for Director of U.S. Arms Control and Disarmament	White House, 2:48 p.m.
22	575–76	Statement Announcing U.S. Grain Agreement Negotiations with USSR	
23	576–77	Radio Address to the Nation on the Death of Federal Diplomatic and Military Personnel in Beirut	White House, 12:06 p.m.
*23	578–79	Remarks at a Ceremony Honoring Victims of the Bombing of the U.S. Embassy in Beirut	Andrews Air Force Base, 6:44 p.m.
*25	579–81	Remarks at Presentation Ceremony for Enrico Fermi Awards at Department of Energy	Forrestal Auditorium, 11:11 a.m.
*26	584–86	Remarks on Receiving the Final Report of the National Commission on Excellence in Education	White House, 4:20 p.m.
26	587–93	Interview with USA Today	White House, 5:08 p.m.
*27	593–94	Remarks to Daily News Crime Fighter Award Winners	New York City, 11:22 a.m.
27	595–600	Remarks and Question-and-Answer Session at Annual Convention of American Newspaper Publishers Association	Waldorf Astoria, 1:04 p.m.
*27	601–7	Address to Joint Session of Congress on Central America	Capitol Building, 8:04 p.m.
28	607	Message to Congress Transmitting the Annual Report on Radiation Control for Health and Safety	
*28	608–9	Remarks Following Meetings with Prime Minister Trudeau of Canada	White House, 1:31 p.m.
28	610	Statement Designating a Representative to Australia-American Friendship Week Celebrations	
28	610–13	Question-and-Answer Session with Reporters on Nomination of an Ambassador at Large to Central America	
*29	615–17	Remarks at the Cenikor Foundation Center	Houston, Texas,

			3:18 p.m.
*29	617–21	Remarks at a Fundraising Dinner for Senator John Tower	Houston, Texas 9:52 p.m.
*30	621	Remarks at a Meeting with the University of Houston Basketball Team	Houston, Texas, 8:58 a.m.
30	621–23	Radio Address to the Nation on Education	White House, recorded for broadcast on April 29

Notes

Introduction

1. Charles Elder and Roger Cobb, *The Political Uses of Symbols* (New York: Longman, 1983), 129. See also 115, 118.

2. Murray, Edelman, "Symbols and Political Quiescence," *American Political Science Review* 54 (September 1960): 695–704; Joseph Gusfield, *Symbolic Crusade* (Urbana: University of Illinois Press, 1963), 243.

3. Peter Hall, "A Symbolic Interactionist Analysis of Politics," *Sociological Inquiry* 42 (1973): 51.

4. Ferdinand Mount, *The Theatre of Politics* (London: Weidenfeld and Nicolson, 1972), 8, 51.

5. Kenneth Burke, *Permanence and Change* (Indianapolis: Bobbs-Merrill, 1965), 367; Sheldon Messinger and Robert Towne, "Life as Theater: Some Notes on the Dramaturgic Approach to Social Reality," *Sociometry* 25 (September 1962): 98–110. The idea is discussed at length in the works of Erving Goffman. See section 1 of the bibliography.

6. Hall, "Symbolic Interactionist," 61. Italics in original.

7. See, for example, Elder and Cobb, *Political Uses of Symbols*, 18–21; Dan Nimmo and James Combs, *Subliminal Politics: Myths and Mythmakers in America* (Englewood Cliffs, N.J.: Prentice-Hall, 1980), 68–71; Gusfield, *Symbolic Crusade*, 246; Murray Edelman, *Politics as Symbolic Action* (New York: Academic Press, 1971), 77, 97; Murray Edelman, *The Symbolic Uses of Politics* (Urbana: University of Illinois Press, 1964), 76, 82, 83, 100.

8. Edelman, "Symbols and Political Quiescence"; Gusfield, *Symbolic Crusade;* Milner Ball, "The Play's the Thing: An Unscientific Reflection on Courts under the Rubric of Theater," *Stanford Law Review* 28 (November 1975): 81–115; W. Lance Bennett, *News: The Politics of Illusion* (New York: Longman, 1983).

9. Richard Fenno, Jr., *Home Style* (Boston: Little, Brown, 1978).

10. Louis Koenig, "More Power to the President," *New York Times Magazine*, 3 January 1965, 7, 42–46, reprinted in *Classics of the American Presidency*, ed. Harry Bailey, Jr. (Oak Park, Ill.: Moore Publishing, 1980), 313.

11. Edelman, *Symbolic Uses of Politics*, chap. 4.

12. James MacGregor Burns, *Presidential Government: The Crucible of Leadership* (Boston:

Houghton Mifflin, 1965); Richard Neustadt, *Presidential Power: The Politics of Leadership*, rev. ed. (New York: Wiley, 1964, orig. pub. 1960). See also Erwin Hargrove, *Presidential Leadership* (New York: Macmillan, 1966).

13. James MacGregor Burns, *Leadership* (New York: Harper & Row, 1978). Burns points out (p. 454) that the leadership he is discussing is "not merely symbolic."

14. Lyn Ragsdale, "The Politics of Presidential Speechmaking," *American Political Science Review* 78 (December 1984); 971–84; John Kessel, "The Parameters of Presidential Politics," *Social Science Quarterly*, December 1977, 418–35; Dante Germino, *The Inaugural Addresses of American Presidents: The Public Philosophy and Rhetoric* (Lanham, Md.: University Press of America, 1984); Theodore Windt; *Presidential Rhetoric (1961 to the Present)*, 3d ed. (Dubuque, Iowa: Kendall-Hunt, 1983); Theodore Windt and Beth Ingold, eds., *Essays in Presidential Rhetoric* (Dubuque, Iowa: Kendall-Hunt, 1983); Roderick Hart, *Verbal Style and the Presidency* (New York: Academic Press, 1984); Roderick Hart, "The Language of the Modern Presidency," *Presidential Studies Quarterly* 14 (Spring 1984): 249–64; William Brown, *The People's Choice: The Presidential Image in the Campaign Biography* (Baton Rough, Louisiana State University Press, 1960); Michael Novak, *Choosing Our King: Powerful Symbols in Presidential Politics* (New York: Macmillan, 1974).

15. See M.H. Abrams, "Symbol," as reprinted in *Literary Symbolism*, ed. Martin Beebe (Belmont, Calif.: Wadsworth, 1960), 18. See also Gusfield, *Symbolic Crusade*, 243; Karl Beckson and Arthur Ganz, *Literary Terms: A Dictionary* (New York: Farrar, Straus and Giroux, 1960), 246, 247.

16. Elder and Cobb, *Political Uses of Symbols*, 29. See also Herbert Blumer, "Society as Symbolic Interaction," in *Human Behavior and Social Processes*, ed. Arnold Rose (Boston: Houghton Mifflin, 1962), 179–92.

17. Gusfield, *Symbolic Crusade*, 245.

18. Burke, *Permanence and Change*, 365ff.

19. Messinger and Towne, "Life as Theater," 33; Erving Goffman, *The Presentation of Self in Everyday Life* (New York: Doubleday, 1959), 15. "A 'performance' may be defined as all the activity of a given participant on a given occasion which serves to influence in any way any of the other participants."

20. See Samuel Taylor Coleridge's definition as cited in Maurice Beebe, *Literary Symbolism*, 19; T.H. Gaster, "Myth and Story," *Numen* 1 (1954): 186; Henry Tudor, *Political Myth* (New York: Praeger, 1972), 17, 124.

21. James Robertson, *American Myth, American Reality* (New York: Hill and Wang, 1980), 11.

22. Germino, *Inaugural Addresses*. Other writers use the term "civil religion." See, for example, Robert Bellah, "Civil Religion in America," *Daedalus* 95, no. 1 (Winter 1967): 1; and Novak, *Choosing Our King*. See also Boardman Kathan and Nancy Fuchs Kreimer, "Civil Religion in America," *Religious Education* 70 (September–October 1975); 541–50; and James Fairbanks, "The Priestly Functions of the Presidency: A Discussion of the Literature on Civil Religion and Its Implications for the Study of Presidential Leadership," *Presidential Studies Quarterly* 11 (Spring 1981): 214–32.

23. Barry Schwartz, *George Washington: The Making of an American Symbol* (New York: Free Press, 1987).

24. See Janet Podell and Steven Anzovin, eds., *Speeches of the American Presidents* (New York: H.W. Wilson, 1988), 13.

25. Fred Greenstein, "What the President Means to Americans," in *Choosing the President* ed. James David Barber (New York: American Assembly, 1974), 130, 131.

26. Samuel Kernell, "Public Support for Presidents," in *Perspectives on the Presidency,* ed. Aaron Wildavsky (Boston: Little, Brown, 1975), 148–81. See also Roberta Sigel, "Images of the American Presidency," *Midwest Journal of Political Science,* February 1966, 123–27.

27. Jack Dennis, "Dimensions of Public Support for the Presidency" (paper presented at the annual meeting of the Midwest Political Science Association, May 1975), esp. tables 2 and 3. Portions of the study were published in *Society,* July/August 1976. Stephen Wayne notes an increase between 1968 and 1979 in public expectations of the president's role with a corresponding decrease in satisfaction with the job performance. "Expectations of the President," in *The President and the Public,* ed. Doris Graber (Philadelphia: Institute for the Study of Human Issues, 1982), 17–38.

28. See John Mueller, "Presidential Popularity from Truman to Johnson," *American Political Science Review,* March 1970, 18–24; Henry Kenski, "The Impact of Economic Conditions on Presidential Popularity," *Journal of Politics,* August 1977, 764–73; Kristen Monroe, "Economic Influences on Presidential Popularity," *Public Opinion Quarterly,* Fall 1978, 360–69; Robert Shapiro and Bruce Conforto, "Presidential Performance, the Economy, and the Public's Evaluation of Economic Conditions," *Journal of Politics,* February 1980, 49–67; Samuel Kernell, "Explaining Presidential Popularity," *American Political Science Review,* June 1978, 506–22; Richard Brody and Benjamin Page, "The Impact of Events on Presidential Popularity," in Wildavsky, *Perspectives on the Presidency,* 136–48.

29. Michael Grossman and Martha Kumar, *Portraying the President* (Baltimore: Johns Hopkins University Press, 1981), 263, 264. See also Stephen Hess, *The Government/Press Connection* (Washington, D.C.: Brookings Institution, 1984), 5.

30. Cronin, *State of the Presidency,* 2d ed. (Boston: Little, Brown, 1980), 96.

31. Ibid., 75–116.

32. Douglas Hoekstra, "The 'Textbook Presidency' Revisited: 1974–1980 (paper presented at the annual meeting of the Midwest Political Science Association, Cincinnati, Ohio, April 1981).

33. Jack Valenti, *A Very Human President* (New York: Norton, 1975), 45.

34. *Scholastic News Trails* (Englewood Cliffs, N.J.: Scholastic Magazines, 10 February 1976).

35. Cronin, *State of the Presidency,* 115; Godfrey Hodgson, *All Things to All Men* (New York: Simon and Schuster, 1980), 15, 16; Theodore J. Lowi, *The Personal President* (Ithaca: Cornell University Press, 1986).

36. Hugh Heclo, *A Government of Strangers* (Washington, D.C.: Brookings Institution, 1977).

Chapter 1

1. *The Public Papers of the Presidents of the United States* (Washington, D.C.: Government Printing Office). The papers are available in annual volumes for most presidents, George Washington to the present.

2. Reagan was so often terms a popular president that his standing in the polls may surprise many readers. Poll results are given in Gary King and Lyn Ragsdale, *The Elusive Executive* (Washington, D.C.: CQ Press, 1988), 295–307.

3. Paul Light, *The President's Agenda* (Baltimore: Johns Hopkins University Press, 1983), 160.

4. Stephen Wayne, *The Legislative Presidency* (New York: Harper & Row, 1978), 102, cites Truman as the initiator. However, Theodore Roosevelt, Taft, Coolidge, and Hoover also gave detailed agendas, although Wilson, Harding, and Franklin Roosevelt did not. See Chapter 5.

5. Ibid.; John Kessel, "The Parameters of Presidential Politics," *Southwestern Social Science Quarterly,* June 1974, 1–24.

6. Light, *The President's Agenda.*

7. Ruth Silva, *Presidential Succession* (Ann Arbor: University of Michigan Press, 1951); John Feerick, *From Failing Hands* (New York: Fordham University Press, 1965).

8. Daniel Boorstin, "Our Only American Ritual," *U.S. News and World Report,* 30 January 1989, 35.

9. Joseph Pika, "Interest Groups and the White House: Comparing Administrations," (paper given at the annual meeting of the American Political Science Association, New Orleans, August 1985), 3, 4.

10. See note 26 in the introduction.

11. Lyn Ragsdale, "The Politics of Presidential Speechmaking, 1949–1980," *American Political Science Review* 78, no. 4 (December 1984): 971–84.

12. The polls are taken from Gallup results in George Gallup, *The Gallup Poll: Public Opinion 1935–1971,* 3 vols. (New York: Random House, 1972); *The Gallup Poll: Public Opinion 1972–1977,* 2 vols. (Wilmington, Del.: Scholarly Resources, 1978); and later volumes of *The Gallup Report.* When more than one poll is reported for the month, the first poll is taken, unless a later poll helps to bracket a speech or event. Events are selected by the author from various chronological summaries and reference volumes.

13. Replicating Ragsdale's model for the three-year terms yields a β coefficient for speech of 1.68, with a t statistic of 2.43. A measure for the events shown in the figures is also significant.

14. Merely regressing presidential popularity on time into the term yields a B coefficient of 0.58, significant at .01. This means that presidents are losing more than half a percentage point a month or about 20 points by the end of the third year.

Chapter 2

1. The category in table 2.1 includes the pronoun used with clear reference to either (1) the nation, (2) the American people, or (3) the president or his administration. It also includes use where the referent is unclear as to which of the above three (or more than one) is meant. An original coding attempt to assign the pronoun to one of the three categories was decided against when it was seen that fewer than 50 percent of the cases could be clearly assigned.

2. Richard Neustadt, *Presidential Power: The Politics of Leadership* (New York: Wiley, 1964), 136.

3. Richard Fenno, Jr., "If, as Ralph Nader Says, Congress Is 'The Broken Branch,' How Come We Love Our Congressmen So Much?" in *Congress in Change,* ed. Norman Ornstein (New York: Praeger, 1975), 277–87.

4. The letter writers are cited once as subject for each letter rather than for each sentence in the letter.

5. Fred Greenstein, "What the President Means to Americans," in *Choosing the President,* ed. James David Barber (Englewood Cliffs, N.J.: Prentice-Hall, 1974), 142–44.

6. H. Ford, *The Rise and Growth of American Politics* (New York: Macmillan, 1898), 368.

7. All nouns or pronouns used as nouns are counted for all American actors, with references counted as many times as they occur in the sentence. The coding follows the scheme used earlier for sentence subjects. See table 2.3 and appendix B. See also note to table 2.4.

8. Specific generals named as advisers are not included with the American soldiers generally but are kept in the category of all other actors.

9. The sample of economic speeches includes one for each president when available in the time period, as follows: 14 June 1951, 15 March 1954, 18 September 1963, 7 October 1971, 29 March 1975, 24 October 1978, 16 August 1982.

10. Roderick Hart, *Verbal Style and the Presidency* (Orlando: Academic Press, 1984), 137.

11. This interpretation is also supported by a computer analysis conducted by Roderick Hart. See ibid. Hart also finds Truman high on a scale of plain speaking and Eisenhower high on abstraction. Nixon is high on colloquial language and human interest, whereas Carter, like Eisenhower, is high in abstraction. The one difference in interpretation is found for Carter, whom Hart finds high on a scale of optimism. The speeches used for Hart's study include minor addresses to groups as well as the major speeches analyzed in this chapter.

12. Robert Sherrill, *The Accidental President* (New York: Grossman, 1967), 174.

13. James Robertson, *American Myth, American Reality* (New York: Hill and Wang, 1980), 29. Italics in original.

14. Ibid., 55ff.

15. Quoted in ibid., 43.

16. See both Garry Wills, *Reagan's America* (New York: Doubleday, 1987), and Michael Rogin, *Ronald Reagan: The Movie* (Berkeley: University of California Press, 1987).

17. Thomas Cronin, *The State of the Presidency,* 2d ed. (Boston: Little, Brown, 1980), 115.

18. Murray Edelman, *The Symbolic Uses of Politics* (Urbana: University of Illinois Press, 1964), 95.

Chapter 3

1. Richard Neustadt, *Presidential Power: The Politics of Leadership,* rev. ed. (New York: Wiley, 1980; orig. 1960), chap. 1.

2. The analysis is based on the same economic speeches reported in table 3.2, for all main verbs used with "we" "the American people," "the nation," or a synonym. The same coding is used for the singular-pronoun analysis with one additional clarification. Description of accomplishments that do not specify a particular result are coded as general statements. (We have held down inflation; we have cut costly programs; we have protected the dollar.) In contrast, we have cut inflation by x amount, we have cut Post Office personnel, we have protected the dollar by x action in the World Bank are coded as specific acts. The verb used with the most frequency, it is interesting to note, is the word "need" (as in you [the American people] need, and we need some particular legislation.) "Need" is coded in the category of general statements and taking positions.

3. Lyn Ragsdale, "Presidents and Publics: The Dialogue of Presidential Leadership, 1949–1979" (Ph.D. dissertation, University of Wisconsin-Madison, 1982), 218, 219.

4. Clinton Rossiter, *The American Presidency* (New York: Mentor, 1956), 38, 173. Rossiter includes political skill as one of the few basic requirements of the office and points out that to be chief legislator, a president must also be chief of party. Neustadt concludes his book with the point that "if we want presidents . . . fully useful, we shall have to pick them from among the experienced politicians of extraordinary temperament."

5. The nonelection-year speeches are taken from 1951, 1955, 1963, 1967, 1971, 1975, and 1983. The election-year speeches are from the year following, omitting 1964 when no address was given by the past president (Kennedy). Omitting Kennedy's 1963 address as well would subtract two references to God and none to politics, bringing the nonelection-year ratio to 28 to 12. The State of the Union addresses appeared the best test of the difference between election and nonelection years, since inaugurals are not given in election years and the economic addresses were too few (a total of 3, including 2 for the Truman administration) in the election years to make a comparison.

6. See Robert Denton, Jr., and Dan Hahn, *Presidential Communication* (New York: Praeger, 1986), 97.

7. Charles Dunn, *American Political Theology* (New York: Praeger, 1984), chapter 6; Robert Alley, *So Help Me God: Religion and the Presidency, Wilson to Nixon* (Richmond, Va.: John Knox Press, 1972); Michael Novak, *Choosing Our King* (New York: Macmillan, 1974), 131–136.

8. The Kennedy and Carter quotations are cited by Thomas Cronin, *The State of the Presidency*, 2d ed. (Boston: Little, Brown, 1980), 75; the Nixon quotation is from Novak, *Choosing Our King*, 44.

9. Dante Germino, *The Inaugural Addresses of American Presidents: The Public Philosophy and Rhetoric* (Lanham, Md.: University Press of America, 1984), 51.

10. See Robert Bellah, "Civil Religion in America," *Daedalus* 96, no. 1 (Winter, 1967): 1; Louis Hartz, *The Liberal Tradition in America* (New York: Harcourt, 1955), 39; Lewis Lipsitz, "If, as Verba Says, the State Functions as a Religion, What Are We to Do Then to Save Our Souls?" *American Political Science Review*, June 1968, 527–35. For a different argument, see H. Mark Roelofs, "Church and State in America," *Review of Politics*, January–February 1989.

11. See Germino, *Inaugural Addresses*, 19–29. See also Alley, *So Help Me God;* James Robertson, *American Myth, American Reality* (New York: Hill and Wang, 1980), 69; William Blanchard, *Aggression American Style* (Santa Monica: Goodyear, 1978); Dennis Brogan, *The American Character* (New York: Vintage, 1956).

12. Ibid., 6.

13. Robertson, *American Myth, American Reality*, 69.

14. Blanchard, *Aggression American Style*, 23–27; see also Germino, *Inaugural Addresses*, 11; and Robertson, *American Myth, American Reality*, 347–49.

15. Blanchard, *Aggression American Style*, 23–27; See also, Margaret Mead, *And Keep Your Powder Dry* (New York: Morrow, 1965), 150, 151; and Gabriel Almond, *The American People and Foreign Policy* (New York: Praeger, 1962), 69–72.

16. See James David Barber's analysis in *Presidential Character*, 2d ed. (Englewood Cliffs,

N.J.: Prentice-Hall, 1977), that positive and negative attitudes toward politics help explain individual differences in presidents.

17. Richard Hutcheson, Jr., *God in the White House* (New York: Macmillan, 1988).

18. Donald Spencer, *The Carter Implosion* (New York: Praeger, 1988).

19. Erwin Hargrove, *Jimmy Carter as President* (Baton Rouge: Louisiana State University Press, 1988).

Chapter 4

1. Joseph Pika, "Interest Groups and the White House: Comparing Administrations" (paper given at the annual meeting of the American Political Science Association, New Orleans, August 1985), 3, 4.

2. Samuel Kernell, "The Presidency and the People: The Modern Paradox," in *The Presidency and the Political System,* ed. Michael Nelson (Washington, D.C.: CQ Press, 1984), 243.

3. See also the results reported in Gary King and Lyn Ragsdale, *The Elusive Executive* (Washington, D.C.: CQ Press, 1988), 268–75.

4. William Lammers, "Presidential Attention-Focusing Activities," in *The President and the Public,* ed. Doris Graber (Philadelphia: Institute for the Study of Human Issues, 1982), 145–71. See also Kernell, "Presidency and the People," 242.

5. Pika, "Interest Groups and the White House."

6. See John Orman, "The President and Interest Group Access," *Presidential Studies Quarterly* 18, no. 4 (Fall 1988): 787–91.

7. Speeches to party groups include Truman's (8 November 1949) to the Women's Democratic Club, Eisenhower's (2 August 1955) to the Bull Elephants Club, Kennedy's (12 May 1962) at a Jefferson-Jackson dinner, Johnson's (24 August 1966) at a Democratic party fund raiser, Nixon's (26 September 1969) to the National Federation of Republican Women, Ford's (29 January 1976) to delegates to the Young Republican Conference, Carter's (18 February 1977) to a Democratic National Committee group, and Reagan's (13 November 1981) at a Republican party fund raiser.

 Speeches to support groups include Truman's (22 August 1949) to the Veterans of Foreign Wars, Eisenhower's (22 September 1953) to the American Bankers Association, Kennedy's (7 December 1961) to an AFL-CIO convention, Johnson's (3 May 1965) to the AFL-CIO, Nixon's (4 December 1970) to the National Association of Manufacturers, Ford's (8 April 1975) to the National Alliance of Businessmen, Carter's (7 June 1979) to the United Food and Commercial Workers Union, and Reagan's (20 March 1981) to the Conservative Political Action Conference.

 Speeches to cross groups include Eisenhower's (24 September 1954) at an AFL convention, Kennedy's (30 April 1962) at a Chamber of Commerce gathering, Johnson's (22 June 1967) to the Jaycees, Nixon's (11 November 1971) to the AFL-CIO, Ford's (22 September 1975) to the AFL-CIO; and Reagan's (1 February 1983) to union employees at a Chrysler assembly plant. Truman gave no minor addresses to cross groups in the years 1949–51.

8. Quoted in Robert Donovan, *Eisenhower: The Inside Story* (New York: Harper, 1956), 71.

9. Michael Novak, *Choosing Our King* (New York: Macmillan, 1974), 263–69.

Notes to Chapter 5

1. James Ceaser et al., "The Rise of the Rhetorical Presidency," *Presidential Studies Quarterly* 11, no. 2 (Spring 1981): 158–71; Thomas Cronin, *The State of the Presidency*, 2nd ed. (Boston: Little, Brown, 1980), 75ff.

2. Dante Germino, *The Inaugural Address of American Presidents* (Lanham, Md.: University Press of America, 1984).

3. William Brown, *The People's Choice: The Presidential Image in the Campaign Biography* (Baton Rouge: Louisiana State University Press, 1960), 144, 145. See also Michael Novak, *Choosing Our King* (New York: Macmillan, 1974).

4. Jeffrey Tulis, *The Rhetorical Presidency* (Princeton: Princeton University Press, 1987).

5. Foreign and economic policy speeches become regular expected addresses only with the modern presidents. The inaugurals, taken from the beginning of the first elected term, include speeches of 1905, 1909, 1913, 1921, 1925, and 1933. To parallel the modern presidents, State of the Union messages are taken from the third year of the first elected term: 1907, 1911, 1915, 1927, 1931, and 1935. Harding, who died before this address could be given, is excluded.

6. William Howard Taft, *Our Chief Magistrate and His Powers* (New York: Columbia University Press, 1916), 140–145; 52.

7. Wilson was the first president since Jefferson to address Congress in person. See John Milton Cooper, Jr., *The Warrior and the Priest: Woodrow Wilson and Theodore Roosevelt* (Cambridge: Harvard University Press, 1983), 226. The shorter State of the Union addresses following Theodore Roosevelt and Taft reflect this change.

8. The address of December 8, 1922.

9. Quoted in Cooper, *The Warrior and the Priest,* 221. It is important to see that Germino's discussion of Wilson, in *Inaugural Addresses* 8–10, deals with domestic policy rhetoric.

10. See Gary King and Lyn Ragsdale, eds. *The Elusive Executive,* (Washington, D.C.: CQ Press, 1988), 190–205. For example, there is a large increase in the average number of full time White House staff in the Truman years, and again for Eisenhower and Kennedy. The trend then stabilizes.

11. Even Colonel House, who did so much as adviser to Wilson, is described as being consulted after the president had prepared a draft. See Alexander George and Juliette George, *Woodrow Wilson and Colonel House: A Personality Study* (New York: Dover, 1956), 123, 187. Truman appears to be the last president to write his own speeches, as he describes several times in his private papers. See Robert H. Ferrell, ed. *Off the Record: The Private Papers of Harry S. Truman* (New York: Harper and Row, 1980), 62, 213, 245. Here are the remarks of the war-time president, after returning from the Potsdam Conference:

    While all this has been going on I've been trying to get ready a radio address to the nation on the Berlin Conference. Made the first draft on the ship coming back. Discussed it with [five people]. Rewrote it four times and then the Japs offered to surrender and it had to be done again. As first put up it contained 4500 words and a thousand had to be taken out. It caused me a week of headaches but finally seemed to go over all right when it was said over the radio at 10 P.M. tonight. (p. 245)

12. In addition to individual biographies, a good source for the composition of speeches by the modern presidents is Carl Brauer, *Presidential Transitions: Eisenhower through Reagan* (New York: Oxford University Press, 1986). Brauer describes how Eisenhower,

"his speechwriters," and several Cabinet members worked on eight drafts of his first State of the Union address over a period of months. (p. 37) He also describes how Carter's speeches, including the inaugural, were "pieced together" from drafts written by people with different points of view. (p. 179). Presidential assistant Theodore Sorensen, *Kennedy* (New York: Harper and Row, 1965), 240, 241, describes the team effort that went into the composing of Kennedy's inaugural.

13. Brauer, *Presidential Transitions*, 31.

14. The first president to be heard over radio was Warren Harding, dedicating a memorial in Baltimore in June 1922. However, the first broadcast of an official presidential address was Coolidge's annual message in December, 1923. In 1923, world series games were also broadcast over a few stations. See Gorton Carruth, ed. *The Encyclopedia of American Facts and Dates*, 8th ed. (New York: Harper and Row, 1987), 461–463.

15. See Brauer, *Presidential Transitions*, 31, 32, who describes Eisenhower's "uneasy" combination of religion and government.

16. Ferrell, ed., *Off the Record*, 241, 245.

17. Richard Fenno, Jr., *Home Style* (Boston: Little, Brown, 1978).

18. Dan Nimmo and James Combs, *Subliminal Politics: Myths and Mythmakers in America* (Englewood Cliffs, N.J.: Prentice-Hall, 1980), 65.

19. Theodore Sorensen, *Kennedy* (New York: Harper and Row, 1965), 240, 241.

20. Roderick Hart, "The Language of the Modern Presidency," *Presidential Studies Quarterly* 14, no. 2 (Spring 1984): 249–64. See also Roderick Hart, *Verbal Style and the Presidency* (New York: Academic Press, 1984).

21. *Ibid.*, 261.

Chapter 6

1. Ernest Griffith, *The American Presidency* (New York: New York University Press, 1976), 216, 217.

2. Richard Neustadt, *Presidential Power: The Politics of Leadership*, rev. ed. (New York: Wiley, 1964), 136.

3. Hugh Heclo and Lester Salamon, eds., *The Illusion of Presidential Government* (Boulder, Colo.: Westview Press, 1981), 292.

4. Thomas Cronin, *The State of the Presidency*, 2d ed. (Boston: Little, Brown, 1980), 115.

5. Novak, *Choosing Our King*, 24.

6. Clinton Rossiter, *The American Presidency*, 2d ed. (New York: Harcourt, 1960), 102, 103.

7. H. Mark Roelofs, "Political Leadership in the Biblical Tradition: Moses, Machiavelli, & the American Presidency." American Political Science Association paper, September, 1989.

8. Alexander George, *Presidental Decision-Making in Foreign Policy* (Boulder, Colo.: Westview Press, 1980); and Irving Janis, *Groupthink*, 2d ed. (Boston: Houghton Miffin, 1982).

9. George Reedy, *The Twilight of the Presidency* (New York: World, 1970), 18, 31.

10. Ibid., 18.

11. Theodore Lowi also makes this argument in *The Personal President* (Ithaca: Cornell University Press, 1987), 104.

12. Peter Hall, "The Presidency and Impression Management," *Studies in Symbolic Interaction* 2 (1979): 296.

13. Paul Light, *The President's Agenda* (Baltimore: Johns Hopkins University Press, 1982).

Bibliography

The bibliography is divided into three sections as follows: Section 1 includes major works on symbolism and symbolic politics. Section 2 is less selective, focusing on the growing literature on presidential symbolism—at this writing, primarily studies of presidential rhetoric and public attitudes. Section 3 is highly selective, citing related books on the presidency, both general works and accounts of presidential-public interaction.

1. Symbolic Politics: General

Anton, Thomas. "Roles and Symbols in the Determination of State Expenditures." *Midwest Journal of Political Science* 11 (February 1967): 27–43.

Ball, Milner, "The Play's the Thing: An Unscientific Reflection on Courts under the Rubric of Theater." *Stanford Law Review* 28 (1975): 81–115.

Beebe, Maurice. *Literary Symbolism*. Belmont, Calif.: Wadsworth, 1960.

Bennett, W. Lance. "Imitation, Ambiguity, and Drama in Political Life." *Journal of Politics*, February 1979, 106–33.

Burke, Kenneth. *A Grammar of Motives*. Berkeley: University of California Press, 1969.

———. "On Human Behavior Considered 'Dramatistically.' " In *Permanence and Change*, 274–78. Indianapolis: Bobbs-Merrill, 1965.

Cobb, Roger, and Charles Elder. "Symbolic Identification and Political Behavior." *American Politics Quarterly* 4 (July 1976): 305–32.

Edelman, Murray. *Constructing the Political Spectacle*. Chicago: University of Chicago Press, 1988.

———. *Politics as Symbolic Action*. New York: Academic Press, 1971.

———. *The Symbolic Uses of Politics*. Urbana: University of Illinois Press, 1964.

Elder, Charles, and Roger Cobb. *The Political Uses of Symbols*. New York: Longman, 1983.

Esslin, Martin. *An Anatomy of Drama*. New York: Hill and Wang, 1976.

Fenno, Richard, Jr. *Home Style*. Boston: Little, Brown, 1978.

Firth, Raymond, *Symbols: Public and Private*. Ithaca: Cornell University Press, 1973.

Frank, Thomas, and Edward Weisband. *Word Politics*. New York: Oxford University Press, 1979.

Goffman, Erving, *Behavior in Public Places*. New York: Free Press, 1963.

————. *Frame Analysis*. New York: Harper & Row, 1974.

————. *The Presentation of Self in Everyday Life*. New York: Doubleday, 1959.

Graber, Doris. *Verbal Behavior and Politics*. Urbana: University of Illinois Press, 1976.

Gusfield, Joseph. *Symbolic Crusade*. Urbana: University of Illinois Press, 1963.

Hoggart, Richard. *The Uses of Literacy*. London: Chatto and Windus, 1959.

Kathan, Boardman, and Nancy Fuchs Kreimer. "Civil Religion in America." *Religious Education* 70 (September–October 1975): 541–50.

Kautsky, John. "Myth, Self-Fulfilling Prophecy and Symbolic Reassurance in the East-West Conflict." *Journal of Conflict Resolution* 9 (March 1964): 1–17.

Klapp, Orrin. *Symbolic Leaders*. Chicago: Aldine, 1964.

Lasswell, Harold. *Psychopathology and Politics*. New York: Viking, 1960.

Lipstiz, Lewis, "If, as Verba Says, the State Functions as a Religion, What Are We to Do Then to Save Our Souls?" *American Political Science Review*, June 1968, 527–35.

Merelman, Richard. "The Dramaturgy of Politics." *Sociological Quarterly*, Spring 1969, 216–41.

Messinger, Sheldon, and Robert Towne. "Life as Theater: Some Notes on the Dramaturgic Approach to Social Reality." *Sociometry* 25 (September 1962): 98–110.

Mount, Ferdinand. *The Theatre of Politics*. London: Weidenfeld and Nicolson, 1972.

Nimmo, Dan. *Popular Images of Politics*. Englewood Cliffs, N.J.: Prentice-Hall, 1974.

————, and James Combs. *Subliminal Politics: Myths and Myth-Makers in America*. Englewood Cliffs, N.J.: Prentice-Hall, 1980.

Novak, Michael. *Choosing Our King: Powerful Symbols in Presidential Politics*. New York: Macmillan, 1974.

Nye, Russel. *The Almost Chosen People: Essays in the History of American Ideas*. East Lansing: Michigan State University Press, 1966.

Roelofs, H. Mark. "The American Polity: A Systematic Ambiguity." *Review of Politics*, Summer 1986, 323–48.

Rosenau, James. *The Dramas of Politics: An Introduction to the Joys of Inquiry*. Boston: Little, Brown, 1973.

Steiner, George. *Language and Silence*. New York: Atheneum, 1970.

Tudor, Henry, *Political Myth*. New York: Praeger, 1972.

2. Presidents and Symbolic Politics

Alley, Robert. *So Help Me God: Religion and the Presidency, Wilson to Nixon*. Richmond, Va.: John Knox Press, 1972.

Blanchard, William. *Aggression American Style*. Santa Monica, Calif.: Goodyear, 1978.

Brown, William. *The People's Choice: The Presidential Image in the Campaign Biography*. Baton Rouge: Louisiana State University Press, 1960.

Ceaser, James, et al. "The Rise of the Rhetorical Presidency." *Presidential Studies Quarterly*, Spring 1981, 158–71.

Dallek, Robert. *Ronald Reagan and the Politics of Symbolism*. Cambridge, Mass.: Harvard University Press, 1984.

Denton, Robert, Jr., and Gary Woodward. *Political Communication in America*. New York: Praeger, 1985.

Dunn, Charles, ed. *American Political Theology*. New York: Praeger, 1984.

Fairbanks, James. "The Priestly Functions of the Presidency: A Discussion of the Literature on Civil Religion and Its Implications for the Study of Presidential Leadership." *Presidential Studies Quarterly* 11 (Spring 1981): 214–32.

Germino, Dante. *The Inaugural Addresses of American Presidents: The Public Philosophy and Rhetoric*. Lanham, Md.: University Press of America, 1984.

Graber, Doris. "Personal Qualities in Presidential Images: The Contribution of the Press." *Midwest Journal of Political Science*, February 1972, 46–72.

Green, David. *Shaping Political Consciousness*. Ithaca: Cornell University Press, 1987.

Greenstein, Fred. "The Benevolent Leader Revisited: Children's Images of Political Leaders in Three Democracies." *American Political Science Review*, December 1975, 1371–98.

———. *Children and Politics*. New Haven: Yale University Press, 1965.

———. "What the President Means to Americans." In *Choosing the President*, edited by James David Barber, 121–48. New York: American Assembly, 1974.

Hart, Roderick, "The Language of the Modern Presidency." *Presidential Studies Quarterly* 14, no. 2 (Spring 1984): 249–64.

———. *The Sound of Leadership*. Chicago: University of Chicago Press, 1987.

———. *Verbal Style and the Presidency*. New York: Academic Press, 1984.

Henderson, Charles, Jr. "Civil Religion and the American Presidency." *Religious Education* 70 (September–October 1975).

Hutcheson, Richard, Jr. *God in the White House*. New York: Macmillan, 1988.

Kernell, Samuel. *Going Public: New Strategies of Presidential Leadership*. Washington, D.C.: CQ Press, 1986.

Kessel, John. "The Parameters of Presidential Politics." *Southwestern Social Science Quarterly*, June 1974, 8–24.

Novak, Michael. *Choosing Our King: Powerful Symbols in Presidential Politics*. New York: Macmillan, 1974.

Ragsdale, Lyn. "The Politics of Presidential Speechmaking." *American Political Science Review* 78 (December 1984): 971–84.

———. "Presidential Speechmaking and the Public Audience." *Journal of Politics*, August 1987, 704–36.

———. "Presidents and Publics: The Dialogue of Presidential Leadership, 1949–1979." Ph.D. dissertation, University of Wisconsin-Madison, 1982.

Robertson, James. *American Myth, American Reality*. New York: Hill and Wang, 1980.

Rogin, Michael. *Ronald Reagan, the Movie*. Berkeley: University of California Press, 1987.

Tulis, Jeffrey. *The Rhetorical Presidency*. Princeton: Princeton University Press, 1987.

Wills, Gary. *Reagan's America*. New York: Doubleday, 1987.

Windt, Theodore. *Presidential Rhetoric (1961 to the Present)*, 3d ed. Dubuque, Iowa: Kendall-Hunt, 1983.

———. "Presidential Rhetoric: Definition of a Field of Study." *Presidential Studies Quarterly*, Winter 1986.

————, and Beth Ingold, eds. *Essays in Presidential Rhetoric.* Dubuque, Iowa: Kendall-Hunt, 1983.

3. Related Presidential Studies

Barger, Harold. *The Impossible Presidency.* Glenview, Ill.: Scott, Foresman, 1984.

Bennett, W. Lance. *News: The Politics of Illusion.* New York: Longman, 1983.

Brody, Richard, and Benjamin Page. "The Impact of Events on Presidential Popularity." In *Perspectives on the Presidency,* edited by Aaron Wildavsky, 136–48. Boston: Little, Brown, 1975.

Cornwell, Elmer. *Presidential Leadership of Public Opinion.* Bloomington: Indiana University Press, 1965.

Corwin, Edward. *The President: Office and Powers.* New York: New York University Press, 1957.

Cronin, Thomas. *The State of the Presidency,* 2d 3d. Boston: Little, Brown, 1980.

Edwards, George. *The Public Presidency.* New York: St. Martin's Press, 1983.

————, and Stephen Wayne, eds. *Studying the Presidency.* Knoxville: University of Tennessee Press, 1983.

Fishel, Jeff. *Presidents and Promises.* Washington, D.C.: CQ Press, 1985.

Fisher, Louis. *The Constitution Between Friends.* New York: St. Martin's Press, 1978.

Golden, David, and James Poterba. "The Price of Popularity: The Political Business Cycle Reexamined." *American Journal of Political Science* 24 (November 1980): 696–714.

Graber, Doris, ed. *The President and the Public.* Philadelphia: Institute for the Study of Human Issues, 1982.

Greenstein, Fred. "Change and Continuity in the Modern Presidency." In *The New American Political System,* edited by Anthony King. Washington, D.C.: American Enterprise Institute, 1978.

————. *Evolution of the Modern Presidency: A Bibliographical Survey.* Washington, D.C.: American Enterprise Institute, 1977.

Grossman, Michael, and Martha Kumar, *Portraying the President.* Baltimore: Johns Hopkins University Press, 1981.

Hart, James. "Presidential Power Revisited." *Political Studies,* March 1977, 48–61.

Heclo, Hugh. *A Government of Strangers.* Washington, D.C., Brookings Institution, 1977.

————, and Lester Salamon, eds. *The Illusion of Presidential Government.* Boulder, Colo.: Westview Press, 1981.

Herzik, Eric, and Mary Dodson. "The President and Public Expectations: "A Research Note." *Presidential Studies Quarterly* 12 (Spring 1982).

Hess, Stephen. *The Government/Press Connection.* Washington, D.C.: Brookings Institution, 1984.

Hilderbrand, Robert. *Power and the People: Executive Management of Public Opinion in Foreign Affairs, 1897–1921.* Chapel Hill: University of North Carolina Press, 1981.

Hodgson, Godfrey. *All Things to All Men.* New York: Simon and Schuster, 1980.

Kellerman, Barbara. *The Political Presidency.* New York: Oxford University Press, 1984.

Kenski, Henry. "The Impact of Economic Conditions on Presidential Popularity." *Journal of Politics*, August 1977, 764–73.

———. "Inflation and Presidential Popularity." *Public Opinion Quarterly*, Spring 1977, 86–90.

Kernell, Samuel. "Explaining Presidential Popularity." *American Political Science Review*, June 1978, 506–22.

———. "Public Support for Presidents." In *Perspectives on the Presidency*, edited by Aaron Wildavsky, 148–83. Boston: Little, Brown, 1975.

King, Gary, and Lyn Ragsdale. *The Elusive Executive*. Washington, D.C.: CQ Press, 1988.

Lammers, William. "Presidential Press Conference Schedules: Who Hides and When?" *Political Science Quarterly*, Summer 1981, 261–78.

Lang, Gladys Engel, and Kurt Lang. *The Battle for Public Opinion*. New York: Columbia University Press, 1983.

LeLoup, Lance, and Steven Shull. "Congress vs. the Executive: The Two Presidencies Reconsidered." *Social Science Quarterly*, March 1979, 704–19.

Lowi, Theodore J. *The Personal President*. Ithaca: Cornell University Press, 1986.

MacKuen, Michael. "Political Drama, Economic Conditions, and the Dynamics of Presidential Popularity." *American Journal of Political Science*, May 1983, 165–92.

———, and Steven Combs. *More Than News: Media Power in Public Affairs*. Beverly Hills, Calif.: Sage, 1981.

Manheim, Jarol. "The Honeymoon's Over: The News Conference and the Development of Presidential Style." *Journal of Politics*, February 1979, 55–74.

Miller, Lawrence, and Lee Sigelman. "Is the Audience the Message? A Note on LBJ's Vietnam Statements." *Public Opinion Quarterly* 42 (Spring 1978): 71–80.

Minow, Newton, et al. *Presidential Television*. New York: Basic Books, 1973.

Monroe, Kristen. "Economic Influences on Presidential Popularity." *Public Opinion Quarterly*, Fall 1978, 360–69.

Mueller, John. "Presidential Popularity from Truman to Johnson." *American Political Science Review*, March 1970, 18–24.

———. *War, Presidents and Public Opinion*. New York: Wiley, 1973.

Nelson, Michael, ed. *The Presidency and the Political System*. 2d ed. Washington, D.C.: CQ Press, 1988.

Neustadt, Richard. *Presidential Power: The Politics of Leadership*, rev. ed. New York: Wiley, 1964.

Orman, John. *Presidential Secrecy and Deception: Beyond the Power to Persuade*. Westport, Conn.: Greenwood Press, 1980.

———. *Comparing Presidential Behavior*. Westport, Conn.: Greenwood Press, 1987.

Ostrom, Charles, Jr., and Dennis Simon. "The President's Public." *American Journal of Political Science*, November 1988, 1096–1119.

———. "Promise and Performance: A Dynamic Model of Presidential Popularity." *American Political Science Review*, June 1985, 334–58.

Paletz, David, and Richard Vinegar. "Presidents on TV: The Effects of Instant Analysis." *Public Opinion Quarterly*, Winter 1977–78, 488–97.

Parker, Glen. *Political Beliefs about the Structure of Government: President and Congress.* Beverly Hills, Calif.: Sage, 1974.

Reedy, George. *The Twilight of the Presidency.* New York: World, 1970.

Rossiter, Clinton. *The American Presidency,* 2d ed. New York: Harcourt, 1960.

———. *Constitutional Dictatorship.* Princeton: Princeton University Press, 1948.

Schlesinger, Arthur. *The Imperial Presidency.* Boston: Houghton Mifflin, 1973.

Shapiro, Robert, and Bruce Conforto. "Presidential Performance, the Economy, and the Public's Evaluation of Economic Conditions." *Journal of Politics,* February 1980, 49–67. See also Kenski comment, same issue.

Sigelman, Lee. "Rallying to the President's Support: A Reappraisal of the Evidence." *Polity,* Summer 1979, 542–61.

———. "A Reassessment of the Two Presidencies Thesis." *Journal of Politics,* November 1979, 1195–1205.

Spracher, William. "Some Reflections on Improving the Study of the Presidency." *Presidential Studies Quarterly* 9 (1979): 71–80.

Stimson, James. "Public Support for American Presidents: A Cyclical Model." *Public Opinion Quarterly,* Spring 1976, 1–21.

Tourtellot, Arthur. *The Presidents on the Presidency.* New York: Doubleday, 1964.

Wildavsky, Aaron, ed. *Perspectives on the Presidency.* Boston: Little, Brown, 1975.

———. "The Two Presidencies." *Transaction,* December 1966, 7–14.

Wilson, Woodrow. *Constitutional Government in the United States.* New York: Columbia University Press, 1980; originally published 1904.

Index

Adams, John, 38
Adams, Sherman, 104
Addresses, major, 16, 18, 19, 21–2, 26–
35, 36, 37, 46, 86, 102–6, 132 *See also*
Economic Addresses, Farewell Ad-
dresses, Foreign Policy Addresses, State
of the Union Addresses
Addresses, minor, 16, 18, 19, 22, 24, 25,
37, 91–106, 132–34 *passim*, 145. *See also*
Groups
Advisers, 14, 17, 46, 47, 48, 52, 131, 134,
143, 144, 146
Agenda, presidential, 20, 35–7, 38, 50,
112, 120, 123, 128
Agnew, Spiro, 146
American Federation of Labor, 93. *See
also* Groups
American military, soldiers, 34, 48, 49,
53, 55, 59, 60, 64. *See also* War
Arthur, Chester Alan, 21

Bay of Pigs, 33
Blacks. *See* Minorities
Blanchard, William, 84–5
Boorstin, Daniel, 23
Broadcasting. *See* Media
Brown, William, 107
Burke, Kenneth, 1, 2
Burns, James MacGregor, 3
Bush, George, 23, 68, 106, 135, 142
Business, *See* Groups

Cabinet: members, 14, 57, 113; depart-
ments, 41; Defense Department, 49
Cambodia, 49
Camp David, 58, 61

Carter, Jimmy, 1, 11, 16, 18, 23, 25, 29,
35, 44, 55, 60, 76, 81, 82, 86, 88, 102,
114, 121, 132, 134, 146; and the energy
crisis, 18, 35; number of major
addresses, 19; foreign policy addresses,
21, 40, 47, 58, 103; polls, public
support, 25, 26, 30, 31; State of the
Union addresses, 31, 52; inaugural address, 23, 40, 47, 63, 66, 75, 116; economic policy addresses, 40, 47, 66, 75,
103; religion and morality, 23, 74, 75,
77, 78, 79, 87, 91, 95, 116; and
Congress, 50, 52, 72; and Camp David,
58, 61; minor addresses to groups, 53,
89–98 *passim*; quoted, 58, 63, 72, 79,
80; and political parties, 66, 91, 92;
farewell address, 147
Chamber of Commerce, 24, 93, 99, 106
Churchill, Winston, 55
Civil rights, 20, 21, 33, 51. *See also*
Minorities
Congress, 10, 11, 13, 16, 25, 34, 36, 37,
38, 41, 47, 50, 69, 72, 110, 111, 113,
131, 139, 140, 141, 143, 144, 145;
presidential addresses to, 19, 20, 21, 34,
43, 52, 92, 112, 120; and political
parties, 16, 34, 53, 61, 67, 131, 132;
mentioned, 6, 22, 25, 45, 68, 73, 80, 87,
109, 121, 124, 127
Congressional, 17, 35, 36, 56, 67, 101
Congressional Budget Office, 55
Constitution, the, 8, 9, 13, 20, 21, 43, 44,
81, 87, 109, 110, 111, 112, 125, 126
Constitutional, 10, 13, 121, 139, 145
Coolidge, Calvin, 9, 113, 115, 119, 121;
inaugural address, 87, 109, 116, 117,

About the Author

Barbara Hinckley has taught at Cornell University and the University of Wisconsin, Madison, and is now professor of politics at New York University. She has been a Guggenheim Fellow and served as vice-president of the American Political Science Association. Her books include *The Seniority System in Congress; Stability and Change in Congress; Coalitions and Politics;* and *Congressional Elections.* She also works as an election consultant for ABC News.